Advance praise for
Love's Journey Home

D0734955

"What a wonderful book _____ tale of love and loss—and love again—to life. Reading it, I felt as if I was right there in the room, experiencing all the sorrow and sweetness, the heartbreak and joy, of real, lasting love."

— Sonia Antaki, author of the *Red Dove* trilogy

"This memoir is full of fast-paced dialog and vivid stories of two lives at its center. It moves from romance to the reality of daily living with another person, and ultimately to the struggle to deal with sickness and death. Touching and beautifully written, it strikes so many chords about love, marriage, and family."

— C. Lee Mackenzie, author of *Shattered*

"A compelling and honest memoir covering the history of a marriage where passionate love is lost and found. *Love's Journey Home* is beautifully written, with insight, compassion, and humor. Each character comes alive on the page demanding respect and sympathy with scenes that evoke both laughter and tears."

— Margaret Rumford, author of *The Life and Times of a Resident Alien.*

"I just loved this wonderful memoir! It's funny in some places, and the way the author just describes love – she did a stunning job. I rooted for her and became enthralled with her love for Jay as if it were a character in the book. I rode the waves with her and was utterly enchanted with every detail that brought me closer to resolution. And when I got there, I hated to close the book."

– Peggy Knickerbocker, author of *Love Later On*

"*Love's Journey Home* is a moving love story, a memoir of a marriage, and a tribute to a caregiver and her patient, who rediscover the depth of their love as the hour of final separation approaches. Gabi and Jay's early romance with its long separations; their 30-year marriage with its passion and extraordinary bond marred by alcohol abuse and emotional absence; and their return to love as the inevitability of Jay's death forces Gabi to face their final separation make for a wonderful book."

– Lori Stewart, author of *Travels With J.J.* and Ceca Foundation's honored caregiver stories

Love's
Journey
Home

a memoir

GABI COATSWORTH

atmosphere press

Published by Atmosphere Press

ISBN (paperback): 978-1-63988-150-5

Cover design by Josep Lledo
Cover photo by Helena Coatsworth

atmospherepress.com

For Jay

Prologue

Saturday, August 23rd, 2014

I stepped out of the car after a four-hour drive and checked out the house. It was missing the pots of flowers that I planted by the front door every spring but otherwise appeared much the same. By the garage, Jay's vegetable garden seemed uncharacteristically overgrown. He was usually on top of every weed and slug, but the cucumbers, tomatoes, and beans were rioting across the ground in cheerful abandon.

Pulling my weekend bag and laptop out of the Prius, I walked into the kitchen and dumped them on the bright-blue counters I'd chosen ten years before, when we built the house. They still looked like new and nothing was out of place, so I guessed my husband had tidied up, knowing I was coming.

There was a stillness to the air inside, as though it hadn't been disturbed for a while. I couldn't see or hear anyone, so I walked through to the picture window in the dining room and gazed at the view. It was still beautiful, the lake serene.

The lawn Jay had planted the year before stretched down to the water, and I could see a few sailboats racing in the distance. A day without a cloud on the horizon.

Jay was lying on a chaise longue on the deck, his eyes closed. A glass of something stood on the low table beside him, sweating in the heat. As I moved forward, I scanned his face, wanting to get used to the idea of being there with him before he saw me. He'd lost weight, and when I looked beneath his tan, there were shadows around his eyes.

"Hi, Jay," I said. His eyelids fluttered open. If all had been well between us, I would have called him Jayway, or darling. But all was not well.

"Thanks for coming up, Gabi."

"No problem."

I'd decided to treat my visit as a weekend in the country and planned to read, swim, and pick blueberries when I wasn't driving my husband to and from his medical appointment. He caught me glancing at his drink.

"It doesn't make the pain any worse," he said, picking it up and taking a sip as though to prove it.

I remained silent.

It had all begun so differently, so long ago.

PART ONE
ROMANCE

Absence diminishes small loves and increases great ones,
as the wind blows out the candle and fans the bonfire
— *François de la Rochefoucauld*

Chapter 1
Romance

London, May-November 1974

I heard about Jay Wilson long before I ever met him. I was twenty-five, newly divorced, and the mother of two small children. I worked for a market research firm in London, part of a global network headed by Jay's company. Among other things, they commissioned the studies that we carried out for a well-known bra manufacturer.

On a lovely day in May 1974, my boss, Dawn, called me into her office. As it happened, Jay's American bra client was in town that week, and Dawn wanted to connect with this lucrative customer. But she had to fly to Copenhagen for the network conference, so she delegated the job of contacting the client to me.

"You're familiar with the projects—you've been working on them. Her name is Cindy Cavallero." She handed me a scrap of paper. "Ring her up at the Hilton and ask her to lunch. You're joining us in Denmark tomorrow, so today's your only chance."

Taking a deep breath, I dialed the hotel and asked for

the client, who answered in an attractive drawl that reminded me of Jane Fonda. She accepted my invitation, and we arranged to meet in the lobby. I was checking my makeup before heading out when the phone on my desk rang.

"This is Jay Wilson. Am I speaking with Gabi Coatsworth?"

I confirmed that he was, liking his voice immediately until he spoke again.

"What the hell do you mean by asking Cindy Cavallero out to lunch?" He didn't even pause for an answer. "She's my client, so *I'm* taking her to lunch. What's more, I'll be reporting your unprofessional behavior to your boss."

As I hung up, I felt my face flush with mortification. I sat in my office, my appetite gone, and my heart sank as I envisioned coming face-to-face with this man in Copenhagen at the network's annual meeting. As the head of it, he would certainly be there.

❈ ❈ ❈

Dawn had arranged for me to attend the gathering, to take the minutes, and to meet people I'd only spoken to on the phone. I'd never been to such an event nor seen Denmark, so, having arranged to leave the children with my mother for a couple of nights, I felt a quick rush of adrenaline as I boarded the plane for Copenhagen. Only my unfortunate phone encounter with Jay worried me, and I mentally rehearsed how I would explain my failure to meet Cindy to Dawn.

Knowing I would meet Jay at the welcome cocktail event that evening, I wanted to feel like a competent businesswoman, not the inept, if not downright shady person he'd spoken to on the phone. So I borrowed a purple dress from a friend. As I checked it out in the mirror before I went down to the party, I felt reassured that I looked like someone who wouldn't let anyone intimidate her.

I was standing near a window on the far side of the room with a glass of white wine, immersed in conversation with a man from the Paris agency. Barely disguising his boredom as he stared through his wire-framed spectacles, he paused and glanced toward the door.

"Voilà," he announced, blowing out a stream of smoke from his *Gauloise*. "The uncouth Yankee has arrived."

I must have looked blank.

"It is Wilson," he explained. "From New York."

I followed his gaze and spotted the man with no trouble. I'd seen his photo in the network brochure, but it didn't do him justice.

Handsome, in what we thought of then as the all-American style, he stood at least three inches taller than anyone else in the room. He was younger than I'd imagined, considering he ran such a big company—I discovered later he was thirty-eight. His blond hair, aquamarine eyes, and pink complexion reminded me of early Technicolor movies.

He wore a blue-and-white-striped seersucker suit, à la Gatsby, and his trousers were too short. We expected this sort of thing from our colonial cousins, knowing they had no dress sense.

Still, his presence commanded attention. The executives in the room may have been talking disparagingly about him only a moment before, but they came forward now, anxious to greet him. He appeared cordial but guarded, and as his eyes scanned the room, they fell upon me. His gaze widened, and I hastily turned my head to continue chatting to my French colleague.

Since Jay had been so rude on the phone, I anticipated he'd be gunning for me again, as soon as he realized who I was, just to drive home his point about not stealing other people's clients.

I managed to avoid him for the remainder of the reception, but when we sat down to eat, I found Dawn and I had been placed at Jay's table. Someone introduced us, and I waited for a critical remark from the annoying American, but he acted as if we'd never spoken before. Grateful, I played my part by providing some relief from business talk, by asking about the wine, people's travel experiences, and the like.

After dinner, the older members of the group excused themselves while the rest of us headed upstairs to the discotheque. It was only a matter of time before Jay asked me onto the floor. As we danced, he told me about his estranged wife and two little girls, whom he clearly doted on.

His trousers might have been too short, but when he clasped me to him, I felt an unanticipated current of magnetism between us. I danced with other people too, but no one was as attractive as Jay.

As the evening wore on, most of our colleagues retired, and only a few of us remained on the dance floor. It must have been well after midnight. From across the room, I saw Jay sitting at the bar, and walked over to perch on a stool alongside him. Apparently, he noticed.

"Do you come here often?" he asked with a grin.

I laughed at this cliché, and explained that I'd never been to Copenhagen before. In fact, we were a few miles outside the capital. I don't know what made me say it. "How would you like to see Elsinore Castle?"

"You mean Hamlet's Elsinore?"

"Yes. They tell me it's not far from here and I have a rental car. I'll bet it's lovely by moonlight."

"Okay," he replied. "Why don't you head out to the parking lot and I'll join you in, say, ten minutes."

I understood the need for discretion, so I nodded, bid the stragglers goodnight, and headed downstairs, my heart pounding with excitement or anxiety—I wasn't sure which.

I was beginning to regret this risky adventure. If people found out I'd spent time alone with Jay, I'd be considered unprofessional, to say the least.

I waited nervously in the chilly evening air, praying none of the Danes who lived locally would catch sight of me as they left to go home. I focused on my breathing, and began to feel calmer, less threatened by Jay's charm, his compelling blue eyes, his smell of soap, and something indefinable that made me lean in to get more of it. My anxiety was waning considerably. Then I spotted a flash of light-colored clothing as he emerged from the side door of the hotel. We got into the car, and I switched on the ignition. Now the die was cast.

"So," I began, turning toward him.

"So," he replied, as he leaned over and kissed me.

I kissed him back, one tiny logical voice in my head telling me this wasn't a good idea. His lips were warm, almost gentle, but the effect was electrifying. Perhaps that was what undid me. He wasn't insistent, which made me want him more. I had to stop. Now.

❊ ❊ ❊

I pulled out of the lot, chattering inanely about Shakespeare and Hamlet, and how interesting it would be to check out the actual location where the story took place. Jay didn't talk much—I barely gave him the chance to.

Soon, the gleaming walls of the Palace of Elsinore came looming out of the dark as the moon floated into view from behind a cloud. We stopped in the empty courtyard.

"May I help you?" came a polite voice. I tilted my head to look up at a royal guardsman who'd materialized next to my window.

"We came to see the castle—is it allowed?"

"The moat is open always, but of course you cannot visit the palace itself until the morning. You must come back then."

"May we just walk around the outside?"

He gave us a knowing glance and nodded.

We walked and talked, telling each other our life stories.

Jay recounted how England had captivated him when he'd lived in London for four years in the early sixties, working for *Reader's Digest*, and spent a year studying at Cambridge. We discovered his elder daughter and my two children had been born in the same London hospital.

I gave Jay the abridged version of my failed marriage to Robin, and told him about Adam, now six, and Helenka, three. He fished out his wallet to show me pictures of his daughters, cute little girls a couple of years older than my children. Girls with mischievous expressions and confident smiles. He told me about Connecticut, where he lived.

He wanted to know where I'd gone to school, and I mentioned Ealing Grammar School for Girls, not realizing he was asking about university. We laughed. We kissed again. And talked some more.

We didn't get back to the hotel until four in the morning.

I managed to get through the next day without falling asleep, though I had to make a painful effort not to catch Jay's eye. He worked things out so we sat together at noon, but he would be leaving the following day, and I might not see him again. I felt a hum throughout my body and persuaded myself it was from lack of sleep.

But thoughts of him buzzed in my brain for days after, making it hard to concentrate on anything else.

Coming back home left me feeling flat as I resumed my day-to-day life. At the office, I kept a sharp lookout for any telex or letter from the United States that might require an answer from me. There weren't any, but I had to help plan a network conference in England, to take place a few months later, which gave me an excuse to get in touch.

I thought I was hiding my feelings by keeping a light,

teasing tone in my communications. I was aware my informality didn't conform to the usual starchy style of British exchanges, but Jay appeared to like it and responded in kind. So, we flirted by mail. Eventually, we were writing to each other daily—I to his office, and he to my home address.

Those of my friends who guessed that I had fallen for him thought I was simply infatuated. But I knew from the beginning that there was much more to it. I recognized something in him as he did in me. Something intangible, yet essential—something immutable. The capacity for love, perhaps.

Our meeting felt like destiny.

❊ ❊ ❊

We agreed to spend some time together after the network conference, which took place a few months later. The meetings and dinners passed without incident, and when the conference ended on Friday evening, I picked Jay up and stowed his suitcase in the trunk of my small second-hand car. At his request, I'd booked a room with a four-poster bed in an old coaching inn, not too far from the airport. The ceiling of our room dipped in the vicinity of the window, as Jay discovered when he bumped into the first low-hanging beam.

He chuckled. "I'm just too big for these old places."

I checked him out. I wasn't looking at his head.

"You certainly are," I said. "Lucky me..."

❊ ❊ ❊

We came down late the next morning, and Jay wanted a traditional British breakfast of sausages (with English mustard, he insisted), bacon, fried tomatoes and mushrooms, toast, and marmalade. No eggs, he explained. He wasn't allergic—he just didn't like them. I made a mental note, adding it to the details of his life and likes I was hoarding.

Breakfast took some time. When asked what he'd like to drink, Jay requested something called Sanka. He drew the line at tea.

"Sir?" The waiter was giving nothing away.

"It's decaffeinated coffee. Like Nescafé, except with no caffeine."

I fixed my eyes on the waiter. *Sorry*, is what I was trying to convey. *He's from America.* The man gave me a sympathetic look.

"I regret, sir," he sniffed, "we don't serve powdered coffee in this establishment."

He intended to put this colonial in his place, I suspected, but Jay seemed oblivious.

"OK. Well, I guess I'll take it regular—and bring some Sweet'N Low, would you?" Catching the waiter's eye, he added, "Artificial sweetener."

I sat there, my second slice of toast uneaten on my plate, beginning to worry about his flight to New York. I stole a glance at my watch. Getting to Heathrow on time would be tough.

I finally exhaled as I swerved around the roundabout marking the airport access road, and slid to a stop in front of Terminal 3. Jay leaned over to kiss me.

"You don't have time for this," I said, attempting to ignore the sudden ache in the center of my chest as I fought off a sense of impending loss.

He opened the car door. "Wait here. I need to do something." And he disappeared into the terminal.

I drummed my fingers on the steering wheel. This cavalier attitude wouldn't wash with British check-in staff, I was sure.

Jumping out of the car, I yanked his suitcase from the trunk and let it drop to the pavement. Then I waited, tapping my foot and trying to appear calm as I scanned the terminal building. What if he missed the plane?

He emerged about ten minutes later and walked toward me at an easy pace, smiling.

"I'm all set," he said.

"You can still make it?" I wondered how on earth this could be possible. Had the flight been delayed?

"Oh, I'll be flying."

I'd known this, of course, but still, my heart plummeted.

"Tomorrow morning." He beamed. "Don't look so worried. It'll be just fine. I'll need to call the office later to say I missed it, but now we can have one more day together. Is that okay with you?" he added, concerned.

I had tears in my eyes. "It's wonderful."

I'd ask my mother to keep the children for one more night. I was pretty sure she would.

I don't remember exactly what we did that day. In the early evening, I drove us out to Richmond, and we walked along the Thames in the fading light, oblivious to the drizzle seeping through the trees overhanging the towpath. I stopped caring about my eye make-up running, because Jay didn't appear to mind. We'd stop and kiss, the only lovers crazy enough to be out of doors in weather like this. We kept walking, hand-in-hand, fingers woven together.

"I used to think love was a word I should never use," Jay said, causing me to stop dead in my tracks. The rain-drenched path beneath my feet had suddenly become unstable.

I didn't dare ask him what he meant. He might mean that love would never be on the cards for us. Though it was already too late for me.

He gazed at me and the towpath returned to its former solid state. "I think I've fallen in…"

I held my breath.

"… Love with you."

I forgot to exhale. Jay pulled me toward him and cupped

my face in his hands.

"I love you too." I hadn't said that to anyone except my children for years, and now the words sounded inadequate. I was swimming in love, not drowning. I was laughing in love, not crying.

Once we'd started saying it, we didn't stop.

Late that evening, as we headed back toward my flat, I asked him, "Would you like to see my children?" I'm not sure why, but looking back, I think I wanted him to know me and my day-to-day life better. Jay had only seen me in business settings or romantic ones, but I needed him to understand something about my everyday world.

"Of course," he said, without hesitation. "I'd love to."

We drove along deserted suburban tree-lined streets to my mother's—all her windows were dark. I expected she'd sleep through any sounds of my coming home at midnight—she'd done so many a time when I was a teenager. By the light of the streetlamp filtering through the glass panel in the front door, we crept up the stairs and into the spare bedroom where the children lay asleep. Jay took in Adam, spread-eagled across the bed, and Helenka, cuddled up under a blanket.

"They're very cute."

I felt a rush of tenderness. Not many men would consider going to see someone's sleeping children on a date. Jay was different.

We ended up back at my flat. He would be flying home the following day, so I slept fitfully, missing him already.

The next morning, while he rummaged in his suitcase for a white T-shirt, I picked up the one he'd worn the day before and held it up to my face, taking deep breaths in.

"Can I keep this?"

Jay's surprised face emerged from the neck of his clean T-shirt as he pulled it on.

"Sure," he said. "But it's kind of ratty. Why don't you take a fresh one? I have plenty."

"This one smells of you." I sniffed it again. "And when you're not here, I want to remember last night."

He came over and hugged me. I burrowed my cheek into his shoulder, needing to feel him close.

By the time I next saw him, I was even more in love with the person I was coming to know from his letters.

"Loving you and being loved by you," he wrote, *"is easily the happiest, most fulfilled, and complete period of my life… has brought me alive in a way I never imagined could happen. You've become the fulcrum of my life, the essence, the reason for my being. You embody the romantic ideal that I had as an adolescent, mentally, spiritually, and figuratively. I now know that romance can be real."*

"I'm wary of reading too much into relationships because I've sometimes been a victim of self-delusion," I wrote back. *"But I feel that I see you and us as we are because we don't need to pretend to be anything that we're not with each other."*

I never stopped to think about whether this person I'd fallen for was real. I was as certain as I could be that we were destined for each other. Perhaps I'd read too many Victorian novels where letters were the main way of expressing emotions, but I trusted Jay and hoped for the best.

❊ ❊ ❊

I was keenly aware of the phantom presence of Jay's estranged wife, Julie, and sometimes tried to picture her in their old farmhouse in Connecticut. I'd never met her in person, but most of my business colleagues were acquainted with her, since she usually accompanied him to the international meetings held in Europe every fall.

Dawn mentioned, seemingly in passing, how delightful, intelligent, and amusing Julie was—perhaps to warn me my romance with Jay would never go anywhere. They weren't divorced yet. In his letters, I read how much he worried about the effect of a divorce on his daughters, whom he adored.

I feared there was no chance for me, but I couldn't will myself to fall out of love.

So, did I feel guilty? Maybe I should have. Yet I wasn't the first woman he'd had a fling with, so I didn't consider myself a homewrecker. I believed him when he told me this was the first time he'd fallen in love. He and Julie had been high school sweethearts, and they were expected to marry after college, so they did.

Knowing from the beginning that our affair was unlikely to survive may have been one reason why I didn't regret it. I was in love and willing to keep loving Jay until there was no hope left. So, I did my best to hold to the moral high ground, asking for nothing he couldn't give me, making no demands.

I had a strong sense that I wanted what was best for the man I loved, even if that might mean giving him up. I only hoped that pain, if it had to come, wouldn't happen yet.

❋ ❋ ❋

Through the months, until the fall, we stayed connected by post. Phone calls were expensive in those days, so we wrote to each other. A lot.

His letters would arrive three to four times a week in the sky-colored airmail envelopes with the red, white, and blue borders. If I was lucky, the postman would come before I left for work, and I'd be able to read them on the train journey in. If not, I'd have to contain my impatience until I reached home.

His words were passionate and full of humor. He responded to my anxieties about my life, my work, or the children—always supportive and encouraging.

"... When you're upset about something, all I care about is letting you know that I'm here, wanting to be leaned on, to help...."

When he signed his letters "I love you," I knew, in my bones and blood, he loved me as surely as I did him. And though I dreaded our inevitable separation, I was conscious, even then, of a deep connection that would always be in my life. To my lasting sorrow, most of the letters he wrote to me back then, which I kept in a locked attaché case, disappeared forever when the case was stolen from my apartment in Evanston, after I came to America.

Decades later, I came across two huge manila folders among Jay's papers, stuffed with the love letters I sent over the six months we poured out our feelings on paper. He'd saved them all for forty years, writing brief comments about the contents on the envelopes alongside the date so he might re-read them in the right order when we were apart. The notes included "religious beliefs," "romantic," "children," "initial fears about us," and even "evergreen honeysuckle," though why he should have thought the latter noteworthy, I don't know. When he answered one of these points, he methodically crossed it through.

I would write to him from my desk at work, stealing airmail stationery from the secretary's supply, until I realized the ink was seeping through from the back, so I could only cover one side. With so much to say, I needed thicker paper.

I'd scribble while I was on the Tube, rattling along the track from Ealing Broadway station to Oxford Circus, my stop. Those scrawled on sheets of paper sometimes ended up too messy to send, but the beat of the rails seemed to repeat, *I love you, love you, love you*—a rhythmic backbeat to my every thought and action.

I made jokes in what I pretended were business communications sent to Jay's office in New York. I addressed all my letters on a typewriter, carefully typing *CONFIDENTIAL*, in capitals, on the envelope, hoping his secretary would think we were negotiating some complicated transatlantic deal. Since mail from me showed up every day, I'm sure she figured it out.

His letters kept me going until I saw him again, a couple of months later. He was slightly rumpled from an overnight flight, his fair hair tidied with his fingers. As he strode from the plane onto the concourse at Heathrow, he paused to scan the gate area for me.

You were allowed to wait there in those days, and I did, not daring to take my eyes off the stream of people coming through. Sleepy parents with excited youngsters, Jewish men with ringlets and wide-brimmed black hats, women in saris, men in dashikis and djellabas, and a tweedy aristocrat or two.

And then he appeared, easy to find, being taller than the rest. Those blue eyes were looking for me, but I saw him first, delaying our meeting by taking the few steps toward him slowly, savoring the moment.

Chapter 2
End of the Affair

We had our last rendezvous in Paris in November. He had meetings there and booked a room at the Hotel Georges V. I blinked as I walked into the enormous gilt lobby from the dark and drizzly street. It was like walking into a lit Christmas tree. I felt out of place among the Chanel and Dior-dressed French women who I imagined were assessing my off-the-peg clothes as I crossed the marble floor to the front desk.

I asked for Monsieur Wilson's room number and the clerk dialed it for me.

"A Mademoiselle Coatsworth to speak to you," he said. Staring in what I thought was a pointed manner, he handed me the receiver.

"Hi." I avoided the clerk's eye. "I'm here," I went on, in case Jay thought I was phoning from somewhere else.

"I'll be right down, darling."

I sat by a potted palm tree, trying to make myself invisible. The scent of Ma Griffe and cigars continued to remind me I was out of my league.

"Is everything okay?"

I smiled as cheerfully as I could, but my shoulders were

tense, and he sensed my discomfort. I tried to improve the smile, but couldn't shake off the premonition that this might be the last time we'd be together.

"Of course," I stood up and smoothed down my coat as he grabbed my overnight bag in one hand, and me in the other, giving me a quick hug.

As we entered the enormous bedroom he'd been assigned, I took in the oriental rugs and antique furniture before stopping at the biggest bed I'd ever seen.

"I thought we could order some room service and stay in," Jay said. "I want to spend every second with you tonight."

The next day, he had appointments, and I whiled away the interminable hours by wandering around a wintry Paris, stopping to drink coffee in a small café, meandering through the Place des Vosges. Many years later, I came to love Paris in the winter, but then it reflected my sense of sadness back to me. Streetlife and sun and flowers had vanished—perhaps they knew my happiness was about to come to an end.

When I heard Jay's key in the lock, I made an effort to look cheerful. He poured himself a drink from the minibar. "Darling, I have a meeting this evening. Remember? I told you when I wrote. Will you be okay?"

"I'll be fine. I'll stay here and read."

"Do you mind having room service again? And help yourself to the minibar. I'll be back as soon as I can."

I didn't feel like eating. I sat in the vast, luxurious room, writing in my journal, trying to get my thoughts to stop going around my head. I wandered over to the little fridge to see what it contained. What would happen if I had a small bottle of champagne? I'd never seen such a thing, but, uncharacteristically reckless, I poured the Veuve Clicquot into a glass flute thoughtfully provided by the Georges V. Then I drank a second split and let myself cry.

I needed a mirror to check my makeup. As I stood up, a feeling of dizziness swept over me. I reached the bathroom just in time to grab the washstand with both hands. I should never have drunk champagne on an empty stomach. When the wooziness subsided, I checked my face again. I looked terrible. My cheeks were red and blotchy. My mascara had run down my face, and my eyes and lips were puffy.

Not wanting Jay to find me like this, I soaked in the enormous tub, filling the room with the exotic scent of the foaming bath liquid. Now my skin glowed a more relaxed pink. My hair still damp, I snuggled into the heavy toweling robe with the hotel crest on it, and sat back on the bed to wait.

The easiest part about being in that room was sleeping beside Jay, breathing in his special essence that stimulated and comforted me. The sheets, even when rumpled with our desperate lovemaking, stayed white and crisp. The pillows remained cool against my flushed cheek.

But I think we both sensed something melancholy in the air. When Jay returned, and we'd made ourselves as comfortable as we could in the circumstances, he initiated the excruciating conversation I'd known was coming. Late that night, we were sitting side-by-side on the bed, not touching, keeping a small, hopeless distance between us. We had to sort this out before we fell asleep.

"I love you more than I've ever loved anyone," he began.

I heard the "but" in his voice, though he hadn't spoken it.

"I love you too." I couldn't look at him.

"Julie asked if I was seeing someone else. She wants to try again."

My eyes widened in shock. I hadn't expected this. Julie had been a shadowy figure to me until that moment.

"What did you say?"

"I told her about you. I had to. When someone asks me a direct question, I always tell the truth."

I moved an inch or two farther away from him to study his face. I saw regret there, and pain. His eyes met mine.

"What did she say?" I didn't really want to hear the answer.

"She wanted to know what I planned to do."

I wasn't going to make this easy for him, so I turned away to take a sip of Evian water from the crystal glass on the nightstand, and remained silent. So did he. Finally, I could stand it no longer.

"We'll have to stop this, won't we?" My voice sounded as though it was coming from far away. I wanted him to deny it.

Jay nodded slowly. "It's mostly for the girls," he said. "They're only six and nine, and they need a dad."

Don't we all, I thought, allowing myself a silent moment of uncharacteristic bitterness. I thought of my own childhood—fatherless since Daddy died when I was twelve. And of my children, growing up without a father too.

"I don't think it's fair to you, either. You deserve to be with someone without complications."

I listened in a trance.

"Julie's a great person," Jay went on. "She's just not you. She never could be."

He reached for my hand.

"I understand," I managed—and I did. I hated what he was saying, but how could I protest when the man I loved was doing the right thing?

I let go of his hand, stood, and, suddenly shivering with cold, walked across the room to the window. Drawing aside one of the heavy velvet drapes, I stared out onto the Avenue Georges V below. The street lamps were reflected in rippled puddles, and a faint rising haze was beginning to obscure the view, turning it into something less real every second. I reached forward and touched the glass. I discovered it was my breath causing the mist. I turned back to find Jay standing behind me. I hadn't heard him approach.

"When?" I whispered.

"I'm supposed to fly back tomorrow, but perhaps I could go a day later."

I began to calculate. Tonight, we'd be here. Tomorrow, the flight back to London. One more night there. So few hours left to share before he disappeared like that view of the street. Not enough. Never enough.

"I don't want to do this," he said, taking me in his arms. "I love you—I don't want to hurt you."

"I know." *And I hate it*, was what I didn't say. "But people always get hurt in this kind of situation, don't they? At least, if your girls can avoid that, it will be something."

He hugged me tighter. "You're wonderful."

I didn't want to be wonderful. I wanted to be with him forever. But all I had was now.

❧ ❧ ❧

Jay arranged to stay one more night in England, and we flew back from Paris to London together. He made a reservation at Le Gavroche, London's most exclusive French restaurant. What else was there to do on our last evening? There was no point in staying at home and crying. Going out somewhere special was all we could think of.

This dinner, this perfect tête-à-tête dinner, would be our final one. He would fly back to America the next day. I understood that if I saw him again, it would be in a business situation where I would have to pretend there had never been anything between us.

I dressed as carefully as I could and reapplied my mascara—washed away in my most recent bout of crying.

We walked through Mayfair, and when we reached the restaurant, its neat bay trees showing the way to the mahogany door, Jay indicated I should enter first. I wasn't sure I wanted to go first. I wasn't accustomed to expensive restaurants and felt awkward announcing us to the maître d'.

"Do you have a booking in the name of Wilson?" I asked. "For eight o'clock?"

"I called earlier," Jay added.

"*Ah. Oui, monsieur.* I have found you. Please follow me."

As we sat down, the maître d' flipped open the white damask napkin and placed it on my lap. I wished he'd go away.

I barely remember that meal. Because I wasn't hungry, I ordered Dover sole, thinking it would be something light. Maybe it was, but halfway through, I put down my fish knife and fork and turned to Jay, too full of emotion to eat any more.

"I will love you always—you know that." I wanted him to be sure.

"Oh, darling," he said, and I saw tears in his eyes.

My own started rolling down my cheeks. He handed me his handkerchief to wipe them away, since sitting side by side made it awkward for him to do it for me.

Our waiter appeared in front of us, a polite frown on his face.

"Is everything all right?" he enquired solicitously. "The sole is prepared to your satisfaction? I can bring Madame something else…."

Why he imagined badly cooked fish could reduce me to tears, I don't know. Did French people react that way?

I shook my head.

Jay managed to eat his steak, by which time I'd succeeded in collecting myself. His handkerchief was covered with my mascara, and I slipped it into my bag as a keepsake. He held my hand under the table.

I think we drank the coffee and nibbled at the *petit fours* that came with it, before paying the bill and stepping outside into the chilly November drizzle. I turned my face to the sky for a moment—even Mother Nature was crying for us. Then I took Jay's arm and huddled into him.

❄ ❄ ❄

We parted the next day, a dark wintry afternoon, for what we were sure was the last time.

I drove Jay to the airport and silently watched him check in for his homeward trip. Everyone else—passengers, airline staff, porters—seemed to be acting so normally. Didn't they know this was the end of the world? I walked him to the departure gate, clutching his hand, knowing I would never be allowed to do so again.

Somewhere along the concourse, he led me over to a window in an empty waiting area. He turned me to face him—then leaned down to kiss me. I clung to him, hoping to imprint his body on mine as tears began to flow. His first, then mine. He took a clean handkerchief from his pocket and dabbed at my cheeks. I ran a thumb under his eye to chase his tears away. The sky over the runways grew steadily darker while we stood and willed time to slow down.

All I wanted was for him to keep holding me. I needed to store up memories for the bleak winter nights ahead.

❄ ❄ ❄

It took a long time before I could think of Jay without longing to be near him. He was three thousand miles away, and there was nothing I could do about it. I felt bereft—the way I had when my father died.

My father, a Polish officer serving in Britain during World War II, had contracted Hepatitis B during the war, through a blood transfusion. By the time I was twelve, my mother was traveling almost daily to visit him in a hospital on the other side of London, which meant my sisters and I were often on our own. I became a responsible child—possibly too responsible for my own good. I was doing my damnedest to make sure my father would come home.

I tried to be helpful and didn't complain when my shoes needed new soles. I simply borrowed my mother's brown army lace-ups and wore them to school for a couple of weeks before mine could be mended.

Daddy died in early June 1961.

My sisters and I were playing in our cousins' back garden. One of us hit a tennis ball over the wall into the next garden just as I heard someone calling us in. I jumped up on the wall and dropped to the other side.

"Come here, everyone," said my uncle, who was visiting from Poland. I didn't want to go inside. I wanted to play forever.

"Just a minute," I shouted. "I have to find the ball."

But there was no way to avoid the truth. When I walked through the French doors and into the gloom of the living room, I saw my mother sitting, stricken, in the wingback armchair, with five-year-old Susan on her lap.

"It's Daddy," she said. I already knew. My sisters were all crying. Somewhere deep inside me, a voice said: "This is what happens when you play."

It took me years to learn it was okay, in fact, good, for me to relax sometimes. I had to learn how to play all over again as an adult. Years later, taking things easy, part of me was always on the alert. At any moment, I expected the piper to demand payment for the tune.

I was unaware of that child inside, who thought she understood the real reason why he'd died, and was busy fixing everything, so she would never have to go through the pain of being abandoned again.

Loving someone could only end in disaster.

I would make no more mistakes. I would certainly never, ever, desert anyone I loved. I would be perfect. I wasn't a perfectionist, exactly. I understood not every*thing* could be perfect, but I believed *I* ought to be.

So, my decisions were designed to ensure no one would leave me. As a teenager, the simplest idea I had was not to date anyone more than once. I'd stand people up or go on one date and then find excuses not to go again. Then, as I began to date more attractive boys, I found some of them hard to resist because they wanted and needed me. They were obviously too stupid to see how imperfect I was.

As if to prove it, in my last year of high school, I met Robin Coatsworth, a darkly handsome man two years older than me, who had a reputation as something of a bad boy. He laid siege to me, and it wasn't long before my defenses fell in response to his undeniable good looks and his persistence. When I found myself pregnant, I married him. After five years of precarious marriage and two babies, I left him and went back to live with my mother, my self-esteem in tatters.

To her credit, my mother never referred to the disaster she'd predicted. She simply allowed me and the children to stay with her while I gathered my wits, found a flat and a full-time job, and, after a while, moved out again to a small three-roomed apartment a few miles away in Richmond, where Jay had first told me he loved me.

Chapter 3
Five Years Apart

The years when I had no contact with Jay were difficult, especially at first. I had my work, which took up much of my time. A small bonus was the fact that it provided second-hand updates whenever he attended the same business meeting or conference as my boss, Dawn.

I was fortunate to have a career I loved, and a great boss. I became accustomed to the idea that a woman could succeed in business, so long as she worked harder than any man in her field, and managed to stay cool in the face of sexist comments and behavior. The fact that Dawn had forged a path ahead of me made my career trajectory easier than it might have been.

I still had to contend with older male clients who thought I was "just a silly little girl," yet felt threatened by me. How else to explain the way they sought to keep me and my fellow women executives in our places? That particular comment had come from a dinosaur at the *Financial Times*, who commissioned readership studies from us.

Though we never discussed this, I think Dawn felt sorry for me, believing I'd been involved in a doomed office romance, though it never felt like that to me. Jay was part of me, and always would be, yet the buoyancy his love had given me became harder to maintain without writing or speaking to him. I missed the physical contact more than I ever imagined I might.

I rarely went on dates since I had few opportunities to meet anyone new. Without the online dating services we have now, I had to rely on social contacts rather than social media. Not many men were interested in a relationship with a single mother.

There was one older man who was, though, and he pursued me for a couple of years. When eventually, he proposed, I said yes, even though I wasn't in love with him. He offered security and he loved me sincerely. Shortly after our engagement, though, wondering what madness had possessed me to settle for less, I broke it off. There would never be anyone to replace Jay.

I was trying to be as good a parent as I could. Working single mothers in mid-seventies London lacked resources for childcare, but I had found a woman not far from where we lived, whose children went to the same school as mine did. So, I paid her to look after Adam and Helenka after school until I picked them up at six o'clock.

She was my only option and very strict about pick-up time. If I ever arrived late, even by a few minutes, she'd look me up and down and threaten to stop taking the kids.

I began to feel like a hamster on the wheel—constantly running to keep up with my own impossible standards of perfection. A part of me always felt someone might die if I failed. One experience almost proved me right.

The afternoon had been full of interruptions, and I hadn't yet learned to say no to any of them. They distracted me from the overdue report I was supposed to be working on. The phone rang, and I swore under my breath, exasperated at one more intrusion.

The caller was my child-minder telling me that Adam

had been hit by a car, and was being taken, unconscious, to the local hospital.

"How is he?" My voice sounded strangely artificial to my ears.

"They're not sure yet, but he's in good hands."

"I'll be there as soon as I can." Part of me couldn't, wouldn't, believe this had happened, but as though on automatic pilot, I phoned my mother—someone would need to take care of Helenka. I cursed the elevator and its slowness as I headed downstairs to my car.

I picked up my mother, who was standing outside her house waiting for me. A veteran of World War II, she handled emergencies without adding to the drama.

"He'll be all right, you'll see. Try not to worry."

Unable to speak, I nodded and tried to believe her.

I kept blaming myself for his accident as I walked through the long hospital corridors to where he lay, motionless, his eyes closed. He looked the way I'd seen him every night of his life as I checked on my children before going to bed myself. Yet not quite the same. His eyes weren't moving beneath their lids the way they did when he dreamed. His arms lay by his sides, instead of flung out above the blankets.

The doctors told me they'd seen no visible injury on his X-rays, and all I could do was to wait until he regained consciousness again.

I sat at his bedside for two days, praying he would wake up from his coma. The nighttime silence remained unbroken, except for the occasional soft tread of a nurse, who'd pick up his wrist and check his pulse against the small gold watch hanging upside down from her apron.

"Any change?"

I shook my head.

"It hasn't been all that long. Don't worry. He'll be fine."

I tried to believe her.

Not knowing what to do with my circling thoughts and

the guilt I kept piling on myself, I found an old romance novel in one of the waiting rooms and attempted to read it. When this distraction no longer worked, I stopped turning the pages and went back to praying for my son.

He woke after forty-eight hours. "Hello, Mum. What am I doing here?"

I was never more grateful for anything. Two days later, he returned home with no apparent ill effects. Yet I continued to hold myself responsible for a long time afterward, my guilt adding to the pressure slowly building in me.

* * *

A few months after Adam had been hospitalized, I'd reached the point of burnout. I had to rewrite a report for the third time because the client didn't like it. Losing Jay, almost losing Adam, and now incapable of doing my job correctly—the combination of these three events brought me to my knees.

I couldn't make myself go to work the following day. I gave the children breakfast, of course, and made sure they were dressed and had their school things. Then I walked outside with them as I did every morning, helped them cross the only road between our house and their school, and trudged slowly back home. We lived in the top-floor apartment of a house converted into two flats. As I reached my front door, I knew I wasn't going to work.

I couldn't raise the courage to phone in, either. What could I say? That for the first time in my life I'd simply hit a wall, reached the end of my tether, come to a grinding halt?

As I undressed and crawled back into bed, I began to understand what all those clichés meant.

No one called me from the office. Or if they did, I didn't

hear the phone ring from my bed, where I'd retreated to avoid the world. Dawn rang the next day to find out what was going on.

"I don't know." I was having trouble articulating the problem. "I just can't rewrite that report again. I don't know how to do it. I've messed everything up. I'm no good at market research...."

She stopped me before I could go any further.

"I'll be over later to pick up the data for the report. I can find someone else to revise it, don't worry. We'll sort out what to do."

A huge sense of relief washed over me as I ended the call and replaced the handset. This was no longer my problem. I put the papers in order and then apprehension began to nag at me. Was she coming to fire me? That must be what she meant. Because who would employ a failure like me?

When Dawn arrived after work, I had the materials ready for her.

"Can I come in? I think we should talk." I saw a concerned look in her eyes.

We sat in my small living room, where I'd tried to give the impression of more space by hanging mirrors on all four walls. It worked, up to a point, except that no matter where I looked, I couldn't escape myself. I wanted a cigarette, but I'd given up a couple of years before. Smoke and mirrors— that was me. Not a proper executive at all.

Dawn listened as I told her how I felt about work and the difficulties of bringing up the children—about feeling too hopeless to manage it all.

"You sound depressed."

In 1970s Britain, only seriously mentally ill people suffered from depression and had nervous breakdowns. Such people would be sent to insane asylums if they couldn't "pull themselves together."

"But…" I began.

"Listen to me. Here's what you're going to do."

I shut up and waited to be told my inferior services were no longer required. Everyone else at the office, apart from Dawn, had degrees in statistics and business. Mine was in Polish language and literature because I'd wanted to honor my Polish heritage.

"You're going to see a doctor tomorrow. Then you're going to take three months off until you feel better."

I couldn't take three months off. What would I live on?

"I'll pay your full salary, and you can keep your company car."

Was I hearing this right? Was she really going to take a chance on me after all this?

"But…" I started again.

"No buts," she said briskly. "After three months—or before if you like—we'll see how you're doing, and you can return to work if you're ready."

I couldn't contain this soup of disordered feelings any longer, and tears began running down my cheeks.

"I'll be off now. Ring me if you need anything. Just get better, all right?"

I never forgot her kindness, nor that she must have gone to bat for me with the board of directors to get their okay to give a junior member of staff three months off, with full pay.

Ten weeks passed before I felt recovered enough to ring the office and ask if I could come back to work.

I'd received a letter from Jay, which I cherished. It was written on stationery from the Hotel d'Angleterre in Copenhagen. It wasn't a love letter. It was simply to tell me that he'd heard from someone that I was ill, but was getting better.

"… *You're a very special person, Gabi, and if there is anything I can do to help, please let me know. Keep your chin up.*"

He signed off with *NFNR*, an acronym standing for

Never Forget, Never Regret, something we'd promised each other. "NFNR. *I never have and never will. Jay*"

I didn't reply. But I treasured that letter and have it still.

Chapter 4
Chicago

I couldn't imagine, then, that answering the phone late on a Friday would change my life.

I'd fallen into a manageable working routine and was sitting in the office on a dark afternoon in January, when the phone rang. No one in my department wanted to pick it up, so I lifted the receiver. It was a client I knew—not because I'd worked with him myself, but because we carried out many studies for his company, which provided packaged vacations to millions of British travelers. He was calling from Chicago.

"This is Richard Maitland-Miller. I'm sitting here in the biggest snowstorm ever." His voice wasn't always clear. Not unexpected on international calls. "I'm in a rented office, and there's no way I'll be able to get back to my flat tonight."

I was puzzled as to why he'd phoned to give me this weather report, but deduced it must be something to do with a project. I made soothing noises because I sympathized, although I couldn't imagine the amounts of snow he was describing.

"There are mountains of it in the streets," he went on.

"I mean, taller than me. People's cars are getting buried."

"Gosh. That must be..." Words failed me. "So, was there something we could help you with?"

"Oh, yes. Right. I need someone to do some surveys out here for me. A few focus groups to find out how Chicagoans think about holidays."

I reached into my desk drawer for my address book. "Here we are. Have you got a pen?"

I gave him the name of a prestigious Chicago outfit and hung up, after wishing him luck in getting through the snow. Google didn't exist yet, so I checked the newspaper for temperatures in Chicago. They were in the twenties. Why on earth did people live there with winters like that?

Then I went home, through a damp, dark, London afternoon, anticipating the birthday cake I'd be sharing with my mother and the children. I was turning thirty.

❋ ❋ ❋

To help our client out, I spent a week in Chicago each month for three months. The company wanted to find out how Chicagoans felt about Caribbean package holidays.

"I would never travel on a holiday if I could possibly avoid it," said one woman in a focus group. We Brits looked at each other in dismay. We might as well not bother trying to sell them our holidays then. We didn't know that an American holiday was a British bank holiday, and an English holiday was an American vacation. We had a lot to learn, and vocabulary was just the beginning of it.

One morning in April, I was sitting in a meeting with Richard discussing future projects in one of the noisy coffee shops at Heathrow Airport. He was leaving for Chicago again in a couple of hours.

This was the terminal where Jay and I had parted five years before, but the memories of that devastation had faded to the point where all that remained was a mild sense of gratitude for the time we'd shared. I had met no one like him since and was sure I never would, so, although I had occasional dates, and one man who wanted to marry me, I never felt able to settle for anyone else.

Richard lit up a cigarette and inhaled. I'd given up a few years before and didn't even like the smell of smoke much anymore. I sipped at my cappuccino. My client was talking about having a market research department in the new company he'd formed, Thomson Vacations.

"I need a researcher to set it up and then run it." He frowned. "And I don't know how to find one. I simply don't have the time to advertise, interview and choose them."

I suggested a couple of names.

"The trouble is, it takes forever to brief them, because they don't understand the Thomson way of doing things," he went on. "Not like you."

He crossed one long leg over the other, took another drag of his duty-free cigarette, and stared at me through his rimless glasses. He must have been in his late thirties, though he looked younger. He'd told me about his wife, Fiona, and three little ones in England. Although busy, he didn't enjoy living alone in Chicago, and was looking forward to his family joining him once he found them somewhere to live.

I don't know what made me say what came next. "I suppose I could come over for a while and help you sort it out."

Immediately, I hoped he'd say no. What was I thinking? I had two children and a job, so the thought of moving to Chicago, whose winters I had just experienced, and where I'd have to arrange schools, childcare, doctors, and who knew what, was ridiculous.

Or—perhaps I could just spend the summer there and sort things out for the company. A few months in America would be an experience my children and I would never have again. My heart was thumping in my chest, but I tried to look as though his answer made no difference to me.

He was silent for a moment. He took a swig of one of the countless cups of coffee he couldn't live without. "Hmm. I suppose I could swing it for six months or so. I'd need to clear it with head office, and you might need a special visa, but the Chicago lawyers could fix that. Do you think Dawn would let you come?"

"If you're serious, I can ask her. Maybe you could write to her too?"

"I expect we could arrange for it to be some sort of consultancy, and your company could invoice us for your services. Then they could pay you..."

He was moving awfully fast, but I knew him well enough by now to understand that he always did. And he usually got what he wanted.

* * *

Six weeks later, in June 1979, the children and I arrived at O'Hare International Airport in Chicago with three heavy suitcases and butterflies in our stomachs. Sitting in the back of the taxi taking us to the leafy suburb of Evanston, the children were silent for a while, staring out of the windows at this new place.

No wonder it felt strange. The topography was completely flat to begin with. London was full of hills—so the horizon was always visible.

On the highway, four lanes of huge American cars that Adam didn't recognize traveled in each direction. I thought fondly of my company car back home, a small gold Renault 5, waiting outside my mother's house for our return.

Once the taxi had turned off the Interstate, Dempster Street, several miles long and dead straight, took us to

Evanston. Strip malls and fast-food places lined the street. Adam looked at them with interest.

"Mummy," he said. "Where are the people?"

I knew what he meant. Downtown Chicago always had people milling around the streets, except in the depths of winter. Evanston looked deserted, now that the students from Northwestern had gone home for the summer.

"They're in the cars," I said. "Shops are quite far apart here, so people tend to drive. There aren't many buses."

"Oh," he said and fell silent.

"We can walk to the beach from our flat," I said to cheer the children up. "We'll be moving in, in a week's time, but for now we'll be staying in a hotel. Won't that be fun? I think they have a swimming pool." I knew they'd like that.

I felt unmoored as we began what we thought would be a six-month stay in the United States. For the first time ever, I had to make a home for my two children and me from scratch. Richard's secretary helped me find an apartment with two bedrooms close to the El station, so I could get to work downtown without a car. It was also opposite the YMCA, so I could swim before work. Across the road stood Saint Mary's school, for the children, who were now seven and ten.

I discovered it was relatively easy to find my way around, given the grid system of streets. The company had provided a rental car for me—a long sleek Ford Fairlane. Parking was never a problem because I could just pull into a space. I never had to parallel park. I was amazed that at a gas station someone would fill my tank, check the oil and clean my windows. Gas was so cheap, compared with Britain, that I never bothered to find out the exact price.

My ex-husband Robin came from England once to visit the children and asked me what the price of petrol was.

Oh," I said airily, "it's either eighty-seven cents or eighty-nine or ninety-one, I think." He looked incredulous. "Of course, the gallons are smaller than ours," I added in explanation.

Robin burst out laughing.

"You idiot," he said in a friendly tone. "That's the octane!"

Since our divorce, we'd stayed on good terms once he remarried and I stopped hoping for any child support payments. I thought it important that the children should see that divorced parents needn't be hostile to each other.

I signed Adam and Helenka up for summer camp at the YMCA, and the school suggested someone who'd look after them until I got home from work. The company paid for the children to fly back to England in July, to see their friends and the family, and for me to collect them when their visit was over. I was enjoying the perks of being a consultant.

On weekends, wanting them to make the most of their American experience, I would take them for exploratory trips in and around Chicago. Downtown, there were the impressive science museum and the aquarium. We drove out of town, too, to the quaint town of Galena on the borders of Iowa, because I wanted to see a hill. Finding an old-fashioned drugstore on the main street, I insisted the children try a root beer float—something typically American we'd only ever heard of. Moe, the ancient proprietor, made it himself at a real soda fountain as we sat on bar stools and watched with interest.

We drove a few miles further, so we could say we'd seen the Mississippi River. We spent a weekend in a log cabin at Starved Rock State Park, and we barbecued Polska kielbasa at the local beach. It wasn't bad but didn't taste like any Polish sausage I knew. I even bought a small portable barbecue, knowing I'd be taking it home with me a few months later.

Fall brought its own learning curve. Having signed the children up for school, I had to get them physicals and a whole lot of school equipment. This had been provided free in Britain, and the physical wasn't necessary there. I knew they could hold their own when it came to English and math. But they knew nothing of American culture or heritage – everything from the Revolution to Thanksgiving and Halloween was new.

Within three weeks, they were speaking with American accents.

"Wait a minute," I said one day, as they asked me to take them for a Big Mac and fries. I had no idea what they were talking about.

"I know you have to talk like that so your friends at school can understand you, but I'm not ready for American children yet. So, when you're talking to me, please talk in English. You can talk in American anywhere else you want."

They still address me with an English accent decades later.

❧ ❧ ❧

I missed my family and friends very much, and even though we wrote to each other several times a week, I might have felt lonely at first, had it not been for Richard, and especially his wife, Fiona. She was about my age and another fish out of water, but since her children were small, she met mothers at the local school. She fostered those friendships and took all the ex-pat families under her wing too.

❧ ❧ ❧

A few months later, I bought a four-poster bed, lace-embroidered sheets, and antique quilts, because by that time Jay was back in my life. When he found out I'd moved to the States months before, he'd written me a friendly letter, typed by his secretary. So, I wasn't even thinking about him as I went on the occasional date and slowly expanded my social life.

It's possible, even likely, that we wouldn't have connected again if I hadn't attended the annual conference of Jay's network, held in Hong Kong that year. Seeing Jay again didn't make my heart beat faster. I asked him if he was happy. He nodded. He and Julie were still married, and she stayed close to him at all the social events, looking a little anxious, though she needn't have worried. I was over him. We'd parted so long ago, and we hadn't exchanged so much as a postcard for five years.

A week or so after I returned to Chicago from Hong Kong, Jay contacted me by letter saying he'd be coming to the Windy City on business and asking me whether I'd like to have lunch. To catch up. Seeing him "just for lunch" was no big deal.

When my office phone rang a couple of weeks later, my secretary picked it up. "Gabi, it's a Mr. Jay Wilson. Would you like to speak to him?"

I would.

"I'm here for a couple of days. Would you like to have dinner?" I still loved Jay's voice. Every time I heard it, I could picture his face, and now I felt vulnerable. I could guess where a dinner with him might lead, and although I still found him attractive, I wasn't about to let him get under my guard when we didn't have a future.

"Oh, sorry." I tried to keep my voice breezy. "I have something on tonight." What I had on was dinner for the children, but I didn't tell him that. "I could do lunch tomorrow."

He was silent for a moment.

"Sure, that would be great. I'm staying at the Hyatt, so..."

I interrupted. "The Marriott's closer to my office. Let's meet there." That hotel was, in fact, a bit further away, but I wasn't ready to meet anywhere near a room to which this man had a key.

I hadn't expected to see him quite so soon. I was dimly aware that our paths might cross again after the Hong Kong meeting, since we were in the same business, but his office was in a former department store in Westchester, New York. Mine, eight hundred miles away, looked over Lake Michigan from the twenty-ninth floor.

Now he and I were sitting across the table from each other for the first time in five years. Outside, a crisp autumn day carried on as if nothing important was happening. We were in the Marriott's crowded coffee shop—the only place that we could get a table. I was surreptitiously looking Jay over as he scanned the enormous lunch menu lying on the table next to his plate. He looked the same as ever, his fine hair still blond and carefully gelled to make sure it didn't flop into his eyes. It reminded me of waking up next to him...

But I shouldn't be thinking of the past now. That way lay disaster. I felt my cheeks redden as he glanced up and caught me.

"Have you decided?" he asked, with a smile.

"Not yet." I left it hanging.

A server was hovering near us. She'd brought Jay's martini and my white wine spritzer a while ago. "Ready to order?"

"Gabi?"

"Oh, right." I was having trouble keeping my mind on the menu. "I'll have the quiche and salad, please."

"Mine's the Chicago strip steak, rare, with a side of onion rings. Thanks."

It occurred to me that he and I had never had a meal in the United States, and I didn't know what he ate on his home turf. He'd written me years before from a "greasy spoon" near his office—that description made it sound perfectly dreadful.

In fact, when I saw it a few years later, it turned out to be a cozy old-fashioned, family-owned Italian restaurant, where he would spend his lunch hours, working or writing to me without being interrupted by phone calls. I'd only ever eaten with him at expensive restaurants in Europe, where he would order foie gras and bouillabaisse with a side order of panache.

I forced my mind back to the present. Jay was asking me something.

"How have you been, Gabi? And how are the children?"

Surprised he'd thought to ask, I told him about how I'd ended up bringing Adam and Helenka to live in Chicago, thinking it would be good for them to experience another culture. We talked about the friends we had in common, but there were things I ought not to ask. He didn't feel any such compunction.

"So—how about your love life?"

This put me on the spot. What might he have heard via the business grapevine? What did he know about me? That three years before, I'd almost married someone else? I'd told Jay there would never be another love like ours, and it was true. Feeling that way, anyone else would be second best, and I might as well settle for less. So, I'd almost married Tom, who was older than me and very insistent. I wasn't ready to explain any of this yet. We were only having lunch.

Though if he was going to get personal, I could, too.

"How about you and Julie?" I asked. "You said you were happy when I saw you in Hong Kong."

"Things aren't ideal, but we were getting along okay, I guess."

Were? I looked at him.

"So, better than before?" We were supposed to be catching up, weren't we?

"I never thought about it until I saw you again and realized my feelings for you hadn't changed."

I dropped my fork—it clattered onto my plate.

What was I to make of this? We hadn't seen each other in so long, and when we'd separated before, I was only twenty-five. Now I was thirty, with a little more experience and more than a little cynicism. I was all too aware how affairs with married men were likely to end, and I wasn't ready to put my heart on the line again.

❊ ❊ ❊

The lunches continued through the summer, whenever Jay came to Chicago. He told his employees he was the only person capable of selling a new survey to agricultural clients in the Midwest, and so his occasional visits became more frequent.

I wondered where all this would lead. I'd planned only to be working in Chicago for another couple of months before I went back to England. By this time, I knew his marriage was in real trouble, and since we'd been apart for five years, I could be certain it was nothing to do with me. It was simply the result of two no-longer-compatible people living together.

"You still love me, you know," he said the next time we met. He stirred some Sweet'N Low into his coffee. "I know because I still love you. You'll have to admit it, sooner or later."

"I do not." I spoke as firmly as I could. "I'm completely over us. It's been five years and I managed just fine without you." I wanted to believe it, but the beat of my heart told a different story. Sometimes it was the beat of apprehension. I would return to live in Britain at some point, and if I let myself become involved with this man, I would simply be setting myself up for the pain of separation again.

But if I turned my back on the greatest love I'd ever known, even though I might have it only for a short time, wouldn't I regret it?

I slept fitfully that night, not just because of the Chicago heat. He was right. I did still love him. He phoned me often after that, and I began to imagine how much I'd miss his calls if they stopped. On his third visit, about a month later, I admitted the truth.

I told him how I'd almost married someone else, but decided at the last minute that I couldn't do it. The truth was, there was never anyone else like Jay.

❅ ❅ ❅

Six months in Chicago had stretched to almost a year, and I began to wonder what would happen to us when my contract came to an end. One day, Richard called me into his office.

He offered me the job as head of a new marketing department, responsible for market research as well as advertising and PR. I blinked, stunned. I'd never anticipated this development.

I called Jay on his private office number. We talked almost daily. My staying in the States hadn't been in the cards, so I wasn't sure how he'd take it.

"That's wonderful, darling," he said. "I'm glad they need you to stay."

I still wasn't sure whether Jay and I had a future together, but I decided I'd have nothing much to lose and everything to gain if I stayed. If I left, I'd lose a unique work opportunity—and our relationship might not survive being on separate continents. I decided to accept the position and see where this new development would take me.

❅ ❅ ❅

Over the months, lunches with Jay morphed into dinners, with predictable results. We were together again. Both of us had business meetings to attend in mid-western cities, and would coordinate them so we'd be there at the same time, even if only for one night.

I was happy then, living in the moment. I didn't know where my life was going, but I had complete faith in our love for each other. That would last, no matter what.

I never had to ask: "Do you love me?" We told each other so all the time.

I was sure that we saw the best in each other and fostered it. Jay's best was easy to love. He was loyal, steadfast, generous, loving, smart, and funny. He didn't mind being teased and considered me his equal, and his best friend as well as his lover. I felt the same.

Neither of us was perfect, but we trusted each other enough to show our bad side from time to time, knowing we'd still be loved. Jay's worst, in my book, was probably his temper, which would explode when he was frustrated. Though he was never angry directly with me, I'd feel myself freezing up in response. Afterward, Jay would explain that his frustration was about life in general, and he'd kick the office chairs to vent his anger. I never became accustomed to these outbursts.

He drank a lot, though he was never drunk. It bothered me, but I felt certain he must be unhappy about his failing marriage, and put it down to that. I was ready to accept I had no experience of the cocktail hour, a daily tradition in his family.

He and his sister Judy were expected to attend—with a soft drink when they were young and a cocktail as soon as they were old enough. It was a time for bonding with his parents, and Jay enjoyed it. His family came from Scandinavian, Scottish, and English stock, with some Irish thrown in for good measure—all legendary drinking cultures.

The three-martini lunch became a cliché of the 1960s when Jay was working in the advertising department of

Reader's Digest and taking clients out for long boozy lunches.

"Dad was famous for having a hollow leg," Jay announced one day, as he poured himself another glass of wine.

I raised my eyebrows.

"He could drink any amount and never show it," he clarified.

I suspect his father may have been difficult to connect with because of his "hollow leg." But Jay kept trying until his father died at sixty-eight, leaving his son to cut short his own career to take over and turn around his father's failing market research company.

The closest my family came to cocktails was a glass of sherry before lunch at Christmastime when the neighbors came to call. So, alcohol was not something I was familiar with.

But since everything else about him was perfect, at least for me, I took his explanation of the cocktail culture at face value, telling myself he'd slow down once we were happily married.

If Jay's failing was his temper, mine was not knowing how to express or even identify my negative feelings, which led to buried layers of resentment. I'd never seen my parents fight. Later, that inability to say how I felt would lead to major trouble.

Life, though, was becoming more complicated. When Julie asked him if he was seeing someone else, Jay, never one to tell a lie, admitted he'd met me again. His wife waited to see whether things would blow over between us, but eventually, she put her foot down.

I'd been in Evanston for almost two years when one day Jay arrived, looking somber. "Darling, we have to talk."

I knew what those words meant—everything was over between us. I fell into the nearest armchair, glad to feel something solid around me. Jay sat across the room.

"Julie has issued an ultimatum."

I felt a cold shiver down my back, despite the early summer heat.

"She wants me to give the marriage one more try."

I guessed I would, too, if I were in her shoes. Jay had asked his wife for a divorce more than once, but she kept hoping they could save their marriage. I said nothing. My mouth was incapable of forming any response.

"She says that any attempt to stay married has no chance of succeeding while I'm involved with you."

My mind was racing. Involved with me? He was my soulmate. Involved just didn't cover it.

"So, she wants me not to see you or contact you for six months..."

Finally, I reacted. I gasped, and Jay raised his eyes from the cigarette he was lighting to calm his nerves. He held up a placatory hand.

"So, how did you answer?" I had to know. Didn't want to know.

Clearly, he had to think about his two girls. They were thirteen and sixteen now, and he loved them.

"She won't admit it's never going to work out, but I do owe her a chance to try. If I do, she won't be able to refuse a divorce."

"Will you write to me?"

I could tell from his anguished expression the answer was no. "No phone calls, no writing, no contact of any kind." He rubbed a hand across his brow. He looked wretched.

I could barely get the words out. "None at all?"

He shook his head. "It wouldn't feel right if I upped and left without doing this for her. If that's what it takes to persuade Julie, I'll do it. Then she won't be able to say I didn't give it my best shot."

He stood up and drew me over to the sofa. Once we were sitting down, he put his arm around me.

"It's only six months. It'll go by fast—you'll see."

I don't think either of us was convinced. I felt rigid with shock.

Those six months seemed like a year. I scoured the trade press for mentions of Jay giving speeches or attending conferences, but the photos of him surrounded by other business people were grainy and small. I carried on with my work and waited. The summer leaves turned to gold and fell from the trees, and the air became sharper as the temperature began to drop.

❋ ❋ ❋

Almost six months to the day, I received a phone call from our Canadian friend, Carl. His company was part of Jay's business network, and they used to go fishing together. He'd checked in with me a couple of times to find out how I was doing, and I guessed he would be reporting back.

"Hello, Carl." A flicker of hope spread through me. "Have you heard from him?" I held my breath.

"Yes, I have. I'm to tell you the waiting is over, and he'll be in touch very soon."

"Oh, Carl." I could feel the tears welling up as I tried to get as much information from him as I could. How was Jay? Did he seem well?

"I can't answer that, but I know he's looking forward to seeing you again."

Of *course* he wouldn't be well, if he was ending a marriage of twenty-one years. Those six months must have been hard on him too. He continued to live with the wife he was going to leave, while trying to make sure his daughters knew he would always love them, that this wasn't their fault.

I couldn't help but have a surge of mixed feelings—happiness and relief, because he and I would be together, and anger I didn't want to admit to, because he'd been out of my life for six months. At that point, sympathy for Jay wasn't one of those emotions.

❉ ❉ ❉

I waited impatiently for Jay's taxi to arrive. He'd phoned me from O'Hare airport to say he was on his way. I'd been worrying that his flight might be late because the wind was blowing hard. The sky was a slate gray, not the brilliant blue I felt it ought to be for such a happy day. I didn't care. I could feel my heart beating a shade faster than usual, in anticipation.

Every time a car slowed in the street, I rushed to the window. After what seemed like ages, the cream-and-green Chicago cab with its black-and-white checkerboard stripe pulled up in front of the house and double-parked. The cab door swung open, and I caught sight of Jay's blond head— a bright spot in the dreary street.

I wanted to watch him while he was unaware of it. I couldn't make out his face since he was leaning through the cab window, paying the driver. He put his hand in his back pocket, where he kept his wallet. Such a familiar gesture. I felt tears pricking behind my eyelids at the thought that I'd be there for all his familiar gestures from now on.

I watched him count out some bills, then he waved a hand at the cab window—telling the driver to keep the change, I thought.

At that moment, he turned and checked out the house. I waved, he saw me, and I went to the front door to catch him running up the steps. He dropped the familiar hanging bag and his briefcase on the porch and opened his arms.

We clung together for a while, not caring who saw us. He smelled the same. He tasted the same. I shut my eyes and breathed in. Then we broke apart. He came into the house and closed the door on the outside world.

Jay held me at arm's length and scanned my face.

"Oh, darling," he said. Then a small frown creased his brow. "Are you okay?"

"Just happy." I blinked hard. "I can't quite believe you're here."

"It must have been hard on you, baby, I know."

No one else had ever called me baby. I knew it was silly, but I loved it.

"I'm so sorry you went through that. But it's over now."

I could see his fatigue, though his smile was still the same.

"Thank God." I smiled back.

He peeked through the archway that led to the living room. I was glad my cleaning lady had been in earlier and left everything sparkling. I could smell the wax polish she used to clean the dining table.

"Where are the kids?" he said.

"Out at their friends'," I reassured him. "We have the house to ourselves until six."

Which would give us a couple of hours.

"Do you want to unpack?" I raised an eyebrow.

Jay laughed. "Oh yes. I've definitely missed unpacking."

He took the hand I reached out to him, and I led him upstairs. My room was at the top of the house, under the eaves. I don't think he noticed that I'd put a small vase of rosebuds in the bedroom, and made the four-poster bed with lace-embroidered sheets. It didn't matter. He was here, at last.

As we were dressing, I scrutinized my face in the oval mirror I'd brought over from England. I didn't appear much different from my usual self, but something was wrong. Why did I feel so sad? He was here, now. I gave my head a shake, thinking it might only be the after-effects of missing him for so long.

Jay caught my eye in the mirror, and I tried to smile.

"What's up?" He rose from the chair where he'd been putting on his socks.

"Nothing. I'm happy, honestly."

He put his arms around me, and I felt my shoulders tense up. What the hell was going on?

He let me go and stepped back to look into my eyes. I slid them away from his gaze.

"Are you mad at me?" he asked.

"No—yes... maybe." I moved a couple of paces away from him, and then told myself not to be cowardly. Jay would understand. I took a deep breath.

"I don't want to be angry with you." I couldn't pretend anymore and burst into tears.

"Oh, baby," he murmured. "I'm so sorry. Come here."

I didn't want to. I wanted him to come to me, so I stayed put. He stepped toward me and held me while I sobbed out all the tears I hadn't cried while he was gone. Now he'd returned, and I let them go. He simply stood there, tall, strong, and solid, kissing my hair from time to time as I buried my face in his chest.

I began to wonder how much Julie had cried when she realized it was hopeless, and whether Jay might be tired of crying women. Whether he'd cried too. Gradually, my tears trickled to a halt.

"I'm sorry." I inspected his chest. "The front of your shirt has mascara on it."

He ignored this attempt at lightening the mood, and stood, holding my hands.

"I'll never leave you again—I promise."

❊ ❊ ❊

Back in Connecticut, where he lived, he moved into a tiny gardener's cottage in the "backcountry" of suburban Stamford, soon nicknamed the Postage Stamp. It stood in the grounds of a much bigger house and I stayed there whenever I flew in from Chicago to visit, which I did every couple of weeks or so, unless he flew out to see me. On

57

alternating weekends, he would see his daughters, Amanda and Heather.

The house was cramped with both of us in it, but serviceable, though for Jay, it was a major change from the spacious antique farmhouse on the water in nearby Old Greenwich, where he'd lived for seventeen years. The cottage stood in a shady part of the garden, which made it quite gloomy inside. He'd furnished it with some cast-offs from his home, and all in all, it took some imagination to see it as a love nest.

We began to make plans to marry a year before we finally did. We told Adam, now thirteen, and Helenka, eleven, and I took them to Connecticut for a week's camping vacation with Jay, so they could get to know him better. It proved to be a rough seven days. Having tried more than once to quit smoking, Jay was convinced that the only way to do it was away from his daily routine and habits. He decided that July 4, Independence Day, 1982, would mark his independence-from-smoking day.

"I can only do it if I'm not in my usual routine," he explained.

Accordingly, at 11:59 p.m. the night before, he stood in the garden of the Postage Stamp and lit his last cigarette. I watched him taking a final puff before stubbing it out on the path.

"Well done," I said, although I had my doubts that he'd keep this up. I knew he'd tried before, and a newly smoke-free Jay was not a man at his sunny best.

Mount Desert Isle in Maine turned out to be lovely, but chilly. We stayed for five nights—the first time the four of us had spent so much time together. I tried eating lobster, one of Jay's favorite foods, but never did become accustomed to the violence necessary to get to the edible part. The children wouldn't even attempt it.

Helenka got a fish hook caught in her leg when Jay took them fishing. He ran over a friend's book when it fell off the roof of the car where he'd left it. He became more cranky as the days went by without a cigarette. We were all glad to get back to Connecticut. One good thing resulted from this trip. As time went by, even though he still responded like a wild animal scenting prey whenever a trace of smoke assailed his nostrils, Jay managed to stay off cigarettes for good. Forgetting his previous failed attempts, he used his success this time as evidence later that he could give up anything cold turkey if the conditions were right.

※ ※ ※

Adam started to suffer from stomachaches a few weeks after we returned from that trip. Looking back, I think it may have been because he finally realized that we would be leaving Chicago for good. So far as he was concerned, we were going to live with an irritable man who enjoyed living in a tent. At the time, though, I simply worried that there was something wrong with my son's digestion.

I took him to see his pediatrician several times, who finally pronounced the symptoms psychosomatic. Adam was unhappy about leaving Chicago, I knew. He had turned fourteen in January, and puberty was causing changes to his appearance and his moods.

Having been a sad teenager myself, I assumed this was part of growing up. I'd grown out of it, I reasoned, and seemed to be okay, after all. It wasn't as if Adam's father had died. In fact, Robin had moved to Florida from Britain, so he was in the same country now. Adam would soon have another dad, which would be great, wouldn't it?

The pediatrician referred Adam to Dr. Rosenbaum, a child psychologist whose sympathetic eyes and short stature made him non-threatening. I made sure Adam kept his appointments, but he couldn't attend very many, since we were to leave for Connecticut in about three months. He did seem to be doing better, so I kept my fingers crossed and hoped I'd be able to give him more attention once we were in our new home.

Chapter 5
Weddings

On the morning of May 7, 1983, I woke in the queen-sized bed in the Postage Stamp. I checked the alarm clock, set for eight. It was only seven-thirty and an hour earlier in Chicago, so my children would still be asleep, for sure. I felt half-excited, half-anxious, about the day ahead. Looking at my soon-to-be husband, still sleeping peacefully, I felt reassured.

We were going to be married at noon, and only we knew about it, apart from the justice of the peace. We decided not to tell our children because they wouldn't be able to be there. We wanted them to attend a ceremony that was joyful, relaxed, and celebratory, instead of a thrown-together wedding which might smack of haste rather than considered judgment.

Adam, Helenka, Amanda, and Heather hadn't even met each other yet, and we thought our hasty wedding might not be the ideal place for them to do so. After a few months in Connecticut, we hoped all of them would be more comfortable with the idea.

❊ ❊ ❊

So why marry in May? Why not wait until later in the summer, by which time the children and I would be living with Jay, and there'd be no need for secrecy? Lawyers.

My work visa was about to expire, and it was not going to be renewed by the US government. The company attorneys insisted that if I were already intending to marry, I should do so before the visa's expiration date so I wouldn't risk deportation. I didn't know enough about American law to argue. The only countries I'd traveled to that required a visa were communist Poland, Czechoslovakia, and Hungary, where jail and deportation awaited anyone who violated *their* travel laws.

Although I found it hard to believe I'd be deported, I couldn't afford to take any chances. Since Jay and I were planning to get married anyway, we decided to go ahead. The only date when I could get to Connecticut for a couple of nights was May 7.

Perhaps the secrecy made it more memorable for us. It was certainly a stress-free wedding.

I prepared carefully for the big day. Feeling I couldn't wear white, because I wasn't that sort of bride, I wore a blue-and-white frock, for something blue. The low neckline was for Jay's benefit, and a sedate sailor collar for mine. I'd found the dress in Chicago after several searches through the racks at Marshall Field's.

The groom sported khaki trousers and a lightweight blazer, and he looked so handsome I could hardly believe he'd soon be my husband. We drank a cup of coffee and ate some of the sticky cinnamon rolls he'd bought the day before to celebrate my arrival. Then we walked outside to pick a spot for the informal ceremony.

I breathed in the fresh morning air and inhaled the scent of lilacs flowering nearby. Alongside them, huge hot-pink azaleas were blooming in the warmth of the sun, and blue forget-me-nots nodded in the borders.

We stood under a cherry tree whose blooms were just about over, and waited for the justice of the peace, Mrs. Ryba, to officiate. After we'd had the mandatory blood test, to check for sexually transmitted diseases and German measles, we went to get a marriage license from her, and she'd agreed to come to the cottage to marry us. She was tall and slim, with spectacles and flyaway hair, and as she read the phrases familiar from so many American movies, I felt as though I were in a movie myself. The landlady and her gardener acted as witnesses.

I didn't have a showy wedding ring, since I wouldn't be able to wear it for a while, and we couldn't afford much, in any case. Two years later, when money wasn't so tight, Jay gave me a gold band studded with diamonds. But right now, we were saving every penny we could to buy the house we'd found, so I made do with the narrowest ring in the jeweler's showcase.

Afterward, we drove into New York for a one-night honeymoon at the Barclay Hotel, where we'd had our first tryst since we met again three years before. We had tickets for *Showboat*, to mark the occasion.

The day after, I flew back to Chicago, taking our secret with me. Only my boss and the lawyers knew about it.

We would keep this May wedding to ourselves for many years, and only celebrated that date privately. I can't even remember how the truth finally emerged, but when the children did find out, they simply shrugged their shoulders as if to say, so what?

❊ ❊ ❊

I left the Windy City for the last time in June of 1983 to move to Connecticut with a moody teenager and his younger sister, who was dying to be an adult too. I thought they'd enjoy the trip on the Lake Shore Limited, whose itinerary promised some lovely vistas. I hadn't reckoned on the fact that the train would travel through the most beautiful scenery at night. Still, with our black cat Bugsy safe in his basket, we arrived at Grand Central Terminal, where Jay met us, all smiles.

Jay and I decided we'd have to have some sort of nuptials for friends and relatives, so they'd know we were officially married. It made sense to do that after we moved to Fairfield and to do so at our new home to save money. Since we needed a couple of months to get the house we'd found into shape, we decided on August 6 as the date and gave our relatives advance notice. I invited my family; my mother and sister Susan made plans to fly over from London.

We'd bought an inexpensive Cape cottage on a hill in Fairfield, on the coast. I loved the idea of being near the sea, although, in truth, we were five miles from town and another mile from there to the beach. This was the first time in years the children and I had settled anywhere so rural.

My first husband and I, with two toddlers, had lived in one of the prettiest villages in England, where my feelings of isolation proved the last straw in our marriage. There was no comparison here. I was older and about to set up home with the love of my life.

Still, we had work to do before we could have anyone over—let alone have a wedding at the house.

The day we married turned out to be a triple-H August day, as the Chicago weatherman would have said. It was hazy, hot, and humid, and we found there was something wrong with the date we chose too. I woke that morning, in 1983, to hear the radio alarm reminding Americans that this was the thirty-eighth anniversary of the day they dropped the bomb on Hiroshima. We looked at each other and agreed not to mention it to our guests. As for us, we weren't going to worry about it—our real anniversary was in May.

After a somewhat cursory snuggle, I made my excuses

and staggered out of bed. My sister was already in the kitchen, slicing carrots and zucchini into matchsticks. We would be catering the wedding dinner at home, to save money.

Jay's best man, Carl, came down from Canada just to make sure we got legally spliced. (He liked to use a nautical term once in a while.) He and I had taken to each other at first sight, so it was a treat to have him with us, holding the groom's hand—metaphorically speaking. He'd spent the night in the local motel—in an air-conditioned room, lucky him—and arrived at the house looking handsome, spruce, and dry. The groom, on the other hand, was sweating over his vegetable garden, picking tomatoes for the Caprese salad Susan and I planned to make.

Having dumped assorted vegetables on the counter, where she was arranging flowers and I was perspiring over cheese on toast to keep people going until dinner, Jay went off to have a shower.

"Is the champagne cooling?" I yelled after him as he left the kitchen. "Yup," he threw over his shoulder and kept going. Truth to tell, it wasn't the real thing. We couldn't afford that, either. I'd bought a Spanish sparkling white wine in elegant black bottles, costing less than ten dollars, hoping this substitute would do. A blind test in *The New York Times* had rated it equal to a top-priced French champagne. Jay didn't care—he thought it a drink for girls, and in any case, would soon switch to martinis—but I felt it wouldn't be a real wedding without it.

Adam and Helenka were off somewhere plotting revenge, I daresay, on this man who dared to marry their mother, thus uprooting them from Chicago, which they'd come to consider home. Jay kept moving our sad collection of furniture around with the idea that everyone would have a place to sit and eat their dinner. Then he found every fan he could muster, plugged them in downstairs, and hoped for the best. My mother followed in his footsteps, making small adjustments to his arrangements.

Susan was doing a wonderfully enthusiastic job of decorating our somewhat sparsely furnished home. She'd driven downtown the day before, on a secret mission, which proved to be the purchase of huge bunches of flowers and yards of white ribbon. She festooned the windows, placed flower arrangements around the house, and decorated the deck, where we planned to hold the ceremony.

She took Adam and Helenka to the nearest plant nursery to find us a gift, hoping, she told me later, to help them feel involved in the day. They returned with a pink rose of Sharon bush, which now stood in its pot, hiding the barbecue. Afterward, we found it a permanent home on the lawn behind the house. I planted one in my Fairfield garden last summer because they always bloom in August.

Jay's daughters, Heather and Amanda, would be coming, along with his mother and her second husband, Harold. Harriet was a formidable woman, whose opinion of me veered between "that woman" (on a good day) and something like "bimbo" on a bad one. Some years later, she would cut Jay out of her will because he'd married me. He didn't care about the money—it was feeling abandoned that completely changed his attitude toward her.

At our wedding, she was polite. Harold held his peace and smiled benignly at everyone. Judy, Jay's sister, was his ex-wife's best friend, but she never made me feel like a pariah. Her husband Gerry was a guy who'd try to infuse life into any drab event, which I daresay they expected this to be.

It was time to get ready. I showered and applied my makeup, cursing the humidity, which made it slide off my face immediately. I wore a lilac silk dress, made from fabric I'd found in Bangkok four years before, without any idea it might one day be my wedding gown. I inspected Adam and Helenka in their 'Sunday best' and gave them a thumbs-up.

We sat around, waiting. My mother fanned herself with

a piece of paper. I felt the butterflies returning to my stomach.

My future in-laws and Mrs. Ryba, the justice of the peace who'd officiated at our first wedding and agreed to "marry" us again, arrived punctually at ten to three. We were all set.

Except, the sky was darkening, and Mrs. Ryba was casting worried glances at the threatening clouds above.

As we stood outside, repeating vows we'd written ourselves, I, too, cast an anxious eye skyward. This was a second marriage for Jay and me, and our children, listening to our vows, looked unhappy, certain this would turn their lives upside down. Just as the justice told Jay he might kiss the bride, a huge clap of thunder announced the arrival of heavy rain. No one had to say this was an omen. We fled into the house in disarray and slammed the windows shut.

❦ ❦ ❦

In the wedding photos, my brand-new in-laws wore skeptical expressions. No church, no real champagne, no friends, they seemed to be saying—how could this relationship hope to last? Amanda and Heather smiled for the camera, but the smile didn't reach their eyes.

The meal wasn't as successful as I'd hoped, either. The filet mignon appeared to be all right, but the vegetables had lost all their color by the time we served them. I'd been trying to impress my new in-laws, but the lack of air conditioning meant the day was too hot for food to resemble the appetizing photos in the recipe book. I wished we weren't having shop-bought cake with fake cream frosting for dessert.

With no A/C, the house became hotter and steamier. The fans offered precious little relief from the humidity, and the temperature was showing no signs of abating. My silk dress was sticking to my back—ties and jackets had long gone.

We were thankful when Jay's family departed, and we were alone, with Carl and my relatives, fanning ourselves uselessly as we sprawled on the furniture, hoping to catch the hint of a breeze. Exhausted, we passed the time debating the merits of humid versus dry heat, without reaching a conclusion.

My "new" husband stood up.

"We need a swim," he announced. "Let's go to the beach."

The sun, if there had been one, had set, and clouds kept scudding across the moon as the remains of the wedding party trod over the sand, swimsuits under our clothes and towels in hand. The man who patrolled the shore wasn't thrilled to find us there, but the clouds were beginning to disappear, and we were newly-weds again, so we didn't care.

Kissing in the sea, then diving and splashing—all of a sudden, life felt very cool.

PART TWO
MARRIAGE

I wondered whether the life that was right for one
was ever right for two.
— *Willa Cather*

Chapter 6
Newly Married

We did have fun after our move to Connecticut—to begin with. While it was still summer, the kids were off school, and I was able to hang out with them. I wasn't allowed to work in the US until I had a permanent resident's card, which would take a year to get. Jay was on summer hours, which gave him Friday afternoons to spend with us.

We shopped for household items, clothes for the children, and back-to-school supplies.

Our realtor introduced us to the Welcome Group, and we joined, hoping to make contact with people who didn't carry the burden of Jay's former friendships. These tended to be couples he'd known with Julie, and mostly lived around Greenwich. Occasionally, he played golf with old buddies at the exclusive club he still belonged to, but we were rarely invited anywhere as a couple. A few months after we were married, he gave up his membership to save money. I didn't appreciate at the time how hard this was for him.

I had no friends at all in my new home, so I suggested the newcomers' gourmet evenings might be a fun event.

We wanted to fit in but didn't belong in any particular

niche. Through the club, though, I met someone who introduced me to two other Englishwomen in town, who took me under their wing. They'd been in Fairfield for decades and were familiar with everything I might need.

We needed doctors for school physicals, dentists, a tree man to do some pruning, a new bank account, insurance, a hairdresser—the list went on. My English friends pointed me in the right direction.

I had so much to learn. Never having been a traditional homemaker, I was sometimes at a loss to know where to start. Before this, all my housekeeping had been done on the fly, so to speak, and my children weren't particularly fussy about how, or even if, I ironed their clothes or cooked their dinners. We couldn't afford laundering for Jay's shirts, so I realized I'd have to do it myself. I didn't mind.

An old Polish aunt had taught me her way of ironing when I was young, and I'd never forgotten. Sleeves first, cuffs and collars last. I bought starch and watched public television as I smoothed away. Try as I might, my efforts weren't up to my husband's expectations. In the end, to my relief, he decided, in spite of the cost, they'd have to go to the cleaners.

I made a schedule for which rooms I cleaned on which day of the week, but the cleaning didn't always get done. I wasn't necessarily at home to do it, because I carried out market research projects for a few travel clients that Jay helped me find.

While I was trying to settle in, I wanted the children to enjoy life in this new place. I'd always taken them to museums, parks, historic homes, and the like. It was something we enjoyed as a threesome, so I familiarized myself with the local tourist attractions.

Some weekends, Jay took us camping, and we would head for a state park with a beach, or, less frequently, to a campsite by the Housatonic River, not too many miles away. Helenka liked sleeping under canvas. She grumbled a bit about having to search for kindling. All she wanted was to put on her new bikini and do nothing, but she seemed to find the smell of pine needles and bacon frying in the open air stimulating.

Adam never took to it, and I began to wonder what I could find for the four of us to enjoy together. On one camping weekend, having directed the children to make their beds, wash up the greasy frying pan and the dishes we'd used for breakfast, and refill the water bottles, Jay stretched and walked down to the riverbank. I followed a few minutes later.

"I think they used to have white water rafting trips along here," he said.

I'd only ever seen white water in pictures, and it didn't immediately strike me as something I needed a closer acquaintance with—rather the opposite. It looked dangerous, not to mention cold. I looked at the river doubtfully.

"It doesn't look very white."

"It doesn't have to be, although that's fun. It's just got to move fast enough to propel a raft along."

The kids, having finished their chores, had wandered up behind us, and I could see a glimmer of interest in their eyes. At last. At that moment, a bright blue inflatable raft, controlled by four young men who looked as though they knew what they were doing, floated serenely by. It didn't look *too* difficult.

Jay caught my eye. "Shall we give it a try?"

The guide at the rental place gave us a safety talk and made sure we were wearing helmets and life jackets, which increased my anxiety rather than diminishing it. How dangerous was this going to be? But I could see Adam and Helenka were delighted with the idea of falling into the river and risking life and limb—and held my tongue.

Someone helped us into a raft and pushed us out into the water, which was flowing relatively smoothly at that spot. Soon, though, we were attempting to shoot the rapids, and I was clinging to the loop handles on the side, praying silently.

The screams I could hear were, in fact, shrieks of delight as water rode over us at regular intervals, soaking us all. Adam, his crew-cut head glistening, was leaning into the river twists with gusto, and Helenka looked as though she'd become a water sprite. Jay, his face furrowed in concentration, was wielding his paddle with enthusiasm and had no time to do anything but keep us moving forward. I just hoped that no one would be thrown from the raft.

The current slowed, and finally, around the next bend, I could see the landing place where we would be able to get out of this mobile death trap. I began to relax.

There was a moment's silence as we scrambled out and stood, trying to get used to dry land again. I looked at these people I loved. They were a mess. Dripping onto the rough grass, wiping the hair out of their eyes as they handed back the safety gear, they appeared subdued. Then I looked at my husband and started to laugh.

Adam looked at Helenka, she looked at me, and Jay looked at his new tribe. The children began laughing too, and so did he, not knowing why. His hair, normally so well-controlled, was stuck to his forehead, and a piece of river weed was plastered to his neck, giving him the air of some preppy water god.

Was this what therapists called bonding? If so, perhaps life as a family might work out.

❊ ❊ ❊

Jay drove us up to Yale to show us his alma mater, of which he was very proud, though sometimes he'd admit ruefully that admission standards were so much higher these days that he'd never get in. But his years there were some of the most important in his life, largely because of the friends he made.

❧ ❧ ❧

Jay had always owned a dog, and since we weren't planning to have any more children, we decided to get one. This was a novelty for me, but I had nothing against them, especially if there were two of us to make sure the animal was walked and fed. McDuff, a Shetland sheepdog, was my idea. I really didn't want a dog that would eat more than I did, I explained—meaning I didn't want to clean up after an animal that consumed more than me. McDuff was friendly and smart, though somewhat confused since everyone gave him different commands. I guess family dysfunction will show up in the family pet, too.

Chapter 7
Children

When we married in 1983, we were hoping for a happy-ever-after life for all of us. Only later did I stop to analyze the consequences of our tying the knot. Particularly for our children.

Amanda and Heather, at sixteen and thirteen, had been devastated when Jay and Julie divorced. After their father left, they continued to live with their mother, and he would see them regularly, sometimes with me, but mostly on his own.

As for Adam and Helenka, they found it hard to make conventional social conversation with Jay's daughters, and after saying hello, would often vanish for a while. My previous entertaining had been with guests they knew and felt comfortable with. Suddenly presented with two new sisters, they didn't know how to relate to these polite strangers.

From the start, Jay's girls never posed their parents a problem, at least, nothing which would cause serious concern. One evening, though, he came home looking worried. I asked him what was wrong.

"I had a call from Julie." He was leaning against the

kitchen counter, sipping at his martini. His face was grave. "It's Amanda."

"What's happened?"

"She's joined the God squad."

I hadn't heard this expression before and assumed it must mean something like the Salvation Army. That didn't seem very likely. His daughter was a senior in high school and surely wouldn't have quit to join a dubious sect.

"She's started going to meetings at the local church."

This didn't sound so terrible to me. I'd been brought up Catholic and had suffered hours of religious instruction. The effect had worn off long since.

"That's the issue?"

Jay nodded. "We can't understand it. We raised her as an atheist. This is just... weird."

I heaved a sigh of relief and tried to keep a straight face. If this was Amanda's idea of rebellion, her parents had nothing to worry about, and I told him so. He calmed down somewhat. It turned out she went there partly to play her guitar in their folk group, and when exams and college applications began to take up more of her time, she eventually stopped going.

Heather, a couple of years younger than Amanda, was quiet from the first. She was someone who felt things deeply and tended to wear her heart on her sleeve. She was in touch with her sadness, and I could tell when she was unhappy. Around her dad, though, she recovered her equilibrium because she loved being with him.

For his part, he was justly proud of them. He never compared them with Adam and Helenka, but I couldn't stop myself from doing so—all the time for the first few years. My comparisons always came out in the girls' favor and only made me feel I'd failed as a mother.

The girls had led a privileged life until the divorce, and Jay was determined to continue giving them the lifestyle they'd known before. He did his best to spend as much time as he was allowed with them. We took them on skiing trips nearby and once to Hawaii with us. My husband promised we'd take Adam and Helenka when they were older. It was partly the expense and partly that, understandably, he wanted to enjoy undiluted time with his girls.

He supported and encouraged his daughters' endeavors and paid their tuition at private women's colleges. He bought them each a secondhand car in their sophomore year of university. His earnings weren't enough for us to save anything, so we took out a second mortgage to pay for their education. He never told his daughters this.

Looking back, I'm not sure how we paid for that trip to Hawaii. Jay always gave the impression he could afford anything, especially when it came to his girls. When we were more financially secure, this was true. At the time, though, it was often a struggle. He was paying alimony and child support, and we had less disposable income than we'd had for a long time.

Amanda and Heather never gave us reasons to worry, though, and I tried to stifle the feelings of resentment their blameless behavior caused. How I sometimes wished for them to do something dreadful, so my kids wouldn't look so problematic by comparison. They never did. They took summer jobs, passed their exams, went to college, and then to Europe for a while afterward, paying for a lot of it themselves.

Knowing they had reservations about me to begin with, I took some of the sting out of the situation by announcing myself as their wicked stepmother when introduced to someone they knew. I figured if I mentioned it first, they'd realize I understood how they might feel, and I think they did. It became a longstanding joke between us. They began to like me bit by bit, and over time we grew closer.

Over the years, I accompanied Jay to parents' weekends at college and, later, graduations. We joined the girls while they were taking their separate trips in Europe. Their father wanted to show them where he'd lived as a young married student in Cambridge, and where his family had spent Christmas in the Cotswolds one year.

Amanda found a job in Boston, not far from where she'd been to college, while Heather stayed closer to home, working in Connecticut. They would spend occasional weekends with us in the cottage we'd bought in New Hampshire, where they'd sleep in the loft bedroom overlooking the wood-burning stove on the lower level.

Jay would tease them occasionally about producing grandchildren for him, which seemed to make Amanda uncomfortable, though she laughed it off.

When Jay first learned she was gay, he was stunned. His sister had inadvertently let the cat out of the bag. He waited for Amanda to come out to him, but she didn't.

A couple of years went by, and she was getting ready to leave for Chicago to study for her MBA at Northwestern University.

"It's not right if she goes away and there's this secret between us." He was pacing up and down the small bedroom of the New Hampshire cottage. Amanda and Barb, "just roommates," were hanging out in the living room below—a last visit before leaving for the Midwest.

"So, what are you going to do?" I asked.

"I don't know."

I had no suggestions to make. This was between a father and daughter. Minutes later, Jay squared his shoulders and went downstairs. I trailed behind, wondering how this would resolve itself.

"Honey," he said, "come and sit on my lap."

Amanda, who was in her early thirties, rolled her eyes but did as he asked, looking distinctly wary. Jay put his arm around her.

"I just want to say one thing to you before you go to Chicago."

She swung a foot, looking as though she'd like to leave

right then.

"No matter what lifestyle you choose," her dad went on, "I want you to know you'll always be my little girl."

He wasn't accustomed to talking about this, and a "lifestyle choice" was the best he could come up with.

There was a moment's silence.

"Oh, Dad." His daughter's voice caught on a sob. "I was supposed to tell *you*, not the other way around." She clasped her arms around his neck, as she must have done so many times as a child, and cried into his shoulder.

"Why didn't you?" I could see the hurt he'd been concealing from her for so long.

She raised her head.

"You remember that time on the Cape? In P-town?"

I did. Provincetown was a popular gay destination, and when we spent an afternoon there, Jay had been shocked at the number of same-sex couples and the public displays of affection he saw. I expect he felt in the minority, which disconcerted him.

"You didn't like being among all those gay people..." said Amanda.

"Oh, honey..." And he hugged her.

Chapter 8
Gardening

I often wondered why a man who worked so hard to control his weekday life liked to spend so much time on the hopeless quest that is gardening. It was an unlikely pastime for someone whose corporate world had him in charge of a company, trying to make it profitable, keeping his employees motivated, and encouraging them to have fun doing it.

But one of Jay's driving forces was the need to provide for his family, whether for those at home or at work. As the years passed, it became clear that, as far as he was concerned, tending a vegetable patch was the same as playing.

Still, Nature insisted on thwarting him at every turn. Enthusiastic weeds would smother neat rows of carrot tops, heavy rains would beat delicate pea seedlings into prostration, or a baking sun would smugly dry out newly set tomato plants. Then there was the Connecticut wildlife, magnetically attracted to Jay's vegetables. Slugs, woodchucks, deer—apparently, they all assumed he was growing this stuff just for them.

The head gardener, as he referred to himself, fought

back. Pesticides, anti-fungal sprays, slug pellets, a chicken-wire fence, and a hose with a timer which he never quite mastered—all were strategically and tactically deployed to vanquish his enemies because Jay loved a challenge, even a battle.

He would walk in from the garden, drenched in sweat, with streaks of earth on his face, where he'd swiped perspiration or a mosquito away. There'd be dirt under his fingernails and on his knees. I daresay he looked like this as a boy, coming in after a morning spent climbing trees or playing in mud puddles.

I'd hand him a glass of water. He'd raise a celebratory fist in the air.

"I've done battle with (fill in the blank)," he would say. "And I have prevailed."

❁ ❁ ❁

Jay came from a generation of men who were expected to be providers—and provide he did. Sometime in late July or the beginning of August, the tomatoes and zucchini would begin to ripen. In the early days of our marriage, I pictured myself in a filmy white dress and a wide-brimmed hat, a ladylike basket over my arm, strolling through the garden and stooping to pick a head of lettuce, a tomato or two, or maybe some fresh peas for lunch.

It wasn't like that, exactly. I would come down to the kitchen in the morning to make myself the first cup of tea of the day, and would pass Jay coming upstairs, looking a bit guilty and distinctly muddy. His gardening uniform consisted of a golf shirt and an old pair of shorts, of which he had an extraordinary collection—madras check, or pink, green, and orange, some with tiny golfers or whales on them. At least he left his earth-filled loafers at the door, but, of course, his feet were covered in dirt, too, which would leave a trail up the stairs. My heart would sink. I knew what this meant.

"Just taking a shower before I get going," he'd say as he paused to kiss me.

In the kitchen, every surface was infested with a plague of tomatoes. Cherry, plum, and beefsteak, as far as the eye could see—and it was a decent-sized kitchen.

He'd been up before me and picked everything he could find. With a sigh—generally followed by a rueful smile—I'd fish out some brown paper bags and start carefully packing the tomatoes into them. His employees would take them and thank him, even if some of the offerings arrived on their desks squashed and they only cost a dollar per pound at the store.

Jay was happy, so long as he'd provided.

Chapter 9
Problems

The exotic flowers our friend Pat Lee sent from Hawaii for our wedding lasted for a month, which was about two weeks longer than our newlywed bliss. I'm exaggerating, but not much. Once the regular household routines of school, business (Jay), and looking for work (me) were established, I had time to take stock of how our happy-ever-after story was unfolding.

In late August, problems started to surface. Jay spent long hours at his office, which I came to learn was necessary to keep the company on track. He rarely brought work home, but sometimes he wouldn't return until after eight in the evening.

Maybe it was because Adam and Helenka eventually realized there was no going back to Chicago and our previous life, or perhaps attending new schools was too stressful. Either way, they began to rebel.

Jay was ready to love my kids—and intended to go on being the same traditional father he'd been with his girls— a loving but strict disciplinarian. His way of parenting had produced two well-behaved daughters, not much older than my children, who never showed any signs of rebellion. My methods were more focused on teaching them independence and street smarts since we had only ever lived in cities. This had resulted in a couple of unruly teens, apparently determined to drive us both nuts. I had no idea how to handle conflict with them, or with my new husband.

The current thinking about stepfamilies recommended the original parent continue to deal with disciplinary issues. Still, it went against the grain for Jay to stand by when the children acted out. He'd told me early on that he thought they needed more discipline. Even worse, I was beginning to think he might be right. So, I attempted to be more firm with them, but felt them retreat from me emotionally, which was hard. Teenagers had to separate from their parents, but this struck me as a particularly tough way to do it.

It didn't take long for things to start unraveling.

Jay was unhappy, and so were they. It made for some intense family discussions, which were supposed to clear the air, but just made things worse. I tried to act as a buffer between my spouse and my kids, but only succeeded in making each feel I was favoring the others. I was constantly apologizing to everyone.

I woke every day wondering what fresh disaster would be laid at my feet, and how I could keep the worst of it from my husband. I was certain that if he knew, he would get so mad he'd give up on the kids and me. As my anxiety levels rose, I was always waiting for the next shoe to drop, hoping that when school started, they'd settle down.

Helenka began attending the public middle school. We'd managed to place Adam at the nearby Jesuit academy, but this turned out to be a mistake. He hated it—the Catholic discipline, the corporal punishment, the snooty students, and the uniform.

I needed to find work. I searched for a few months before British Airways offered me a position in their Manhattan office. At last, I felt we might manage to live without financial anxiety. Still, I had the feeling Jay wasn't completely thrilled about my new position.

"It'll be nice not to have to worry about money, don't you think?" I focused on the positive. "This should improve our cash flow quite a bit."

He sipped at a martini and gave me an odd look. I'd assumed he'd be pleased.

"I don't think you appreciate the way I've provided for you," he said.

I was astonished. That Jay might feel he had to be the only breadwinner hadn't ever occurred to me. I expected to be part of a bread-winning team. I was used to being in charge of my finances, and based on my experience, didn't trust any man to do that for me.

Jay had grown up with an optimistic outlook on money—and a conviction that his role, as the man of the house, was to provide everything his family might want or need. Much of his self-esteem was tied up in this idea of himself as a successful man who could take care of his tribe.

I found, though, that he was often cavalier about paying bills. This was a man who'd never had his phone cut off for non-payment (unlike me in my first marriage), and he was frequently late sending a check.

"They know I'm good for it," he'd say. I wasn't convinced.

Meanwhile, I was the one fielding calls from various utility companies threatening to discontinue service. I suggested it might make his life easier if I took care of writing out the checks. So, Jay gave me a monthly allowance. This wasn't the kind of shared responsibility or equality I'd hoped for.

It was clear to me that finding a middle road would be challenging. So, although my job relieved some of the financial stress, it made other stresses worse.

I found my heart racing sometimes, and went to see a doctor, who diagnosed stress-induced arrhythmia and high blood pressure. I thought this was simply the price I would have to pay for trying to be perfect and decided it would be worth it because of the financial benefit.

But it was no help with the children.

They were in high school by now, and I couldn't justify a babysitter, so they wandered around town after school or hung out with friends, some of whom were rebels too, though we didn't know the extent of it.

No one in my world was happy, and I assumed it was all my fault. God knows, I tried to help everyone, to listen to them, and to advise, encourage, mediate, and support those around me. No one thought to tell me that this was, in fact, an impossible goal. Naturally, I kept failing. I was heading for burnout again if I didn't do something.

I left British Airways feeling nothing but relief. Wanting to be more available for Adam and Helenka again, I started a one-woman company, working from home, representing smaller travel companies based in Britain.

But my dreams of a happy family were about to come crashing down around my ears because by now, I saw how badly Adam and Helenka were acting out. Drinking, smoking pot, and cutting school were just the tip of the iceberg, though I didn't know the details until many years later.

Perhaps they were behaving as many young people do, but neither Jay nor I had any experience of this. When we were young, our ways of rebelling were nothing like as harmful as the ones my children chose.

I was getting close to the end of my tether. We tried counseling—individual therapy for me and both of us with the kids. The children only became harder to handle.

Adam, now seventeen, refused to quit marijuana, which we'd laid down as a condition of his living with us. I could tell he was depressed, and sometimes "pulling all-nighters," but I thought this was just something all teenagers did. No one saw he was suffering from the beginnings of bipolar disorder, not even the professionals, because marijuana masked the symptoms. Unwilling to do what we wanted, he went to visit his father, who was living in Florida with his second wife.

When I realized Adam had no plans to come back, I flew to Fort Lauderdale to see him. Sitting across from my first husband, Robin, in his small kitchen, I watched my ex pour Scotch into his morning coffee, something we'd joked about when we were young marrieds. "If you ever start pouring booze on your morning cereal, we'll know you're an alcoholic," I'd commented, thinking this was the sort of joke any wife might make. Now I had no doubt that's what he'd become.

If, before that visit, I'd thought he might be a disastrous role model for Adam, now I was certain of it.

And I was powerless to do anything about the situation.

❖ ❖ ❖

I came back to Fairfield to find Jay relieved Adam was no longer our problem. His lack of sympathy for my loss contributed to my feeling overwhelmed by a sense of sadness and depression I'd never experienced before. I would cry at unexpected moments, sometimes sobbing uncontrollably at my desk.

I cried for my boy, and unknowingly, for my father too. Huddled on the floor of the bathroom, where no one would hear me, I howled until I was exhausted. I let out my sorrow when Jay wasn't around, so he wouldn't see my unhappiness. Still, part of me believed my marriage to him had resulted in the second major abandonment of my life. In searching for my own happiness, I had lost my son.

Someone suggested I go to Al-Anon, the twelve-step program for families of alcoholics and other addicted people. After all, Robin and Adam were both problem drinkers.

I sat in meetings, none of them in the traditional gloomy church basements I'd seen in movies. Our local churches offered sunny rooms, which ought to have made me feel more cheerful. I listened to the other members, mostly suburban women like me, with tears rolling down my face. Before long, I came to realize that although Adam's problems had turned my world upside down, the people in the rooms were also describing Jay's behavior around alcohol.

There seemed to be many varieties of alcoholics. Some were permanently drunk to some degree and lost jobs, destroyed their marriages, and behaved recklessly. Others lived seemingly well-ordered lives with no discernible side effects, yet were dependent on their daily fix to get through it. Jay fell into the latter category, which was one reason it took me so long to figure it out.

I thought about the two men I'd married. What was wrong with me? How could I have married not one, but two, problem drinkers?

I immediately understood that Adam had moved beyond my sphere of influence. But I thought if Jay realized how distressed I was, something might change.

With Adam gone, Helenka became the focus of my worries. At first, I was relieved that her rebellion took the form of getting multiple ear piercings, dying her hair blond, and adopting a short punk-rocker haircut. If that was the extent of it, I ought to be able to cope.

But she began flouting curfew, hanging out with older kids, and dating boys she refused to talk about, never mind bring home. Smoking pot and cigarettes were almost a given by now, and soon I received phone calls from her teachers, asking why we hadn't responded to their notifications of her truancy. They'd been intercepted by Helenka, of course.

We tried everything we could to make her behave. We told her she was grounded. We stopped her allowance. She couldn't see her friends. All of this only served to make the situation worse. She and I screamed at each other. Having repressed my feelings for so long, I, the so-called rational adult, was incapable of expressing how I felt in any other way. This only happened when Jay wasn't at home, of course, because we both knew how angry he would be at her mistreatment of me. Afterward, I felt ashamed of my loss of control, too mortified to tell anyone about it.

Finally, Helenka announced she wanted to go away to boarding school since life at home was so awful. It turned out to be the right thing for her. She was happy to go and loved her time there.

I felt guilty—and relieved. Maybe Jay and I would have a chance to return to the loving people we'd once been. I didn't reckon with the fact that when the children chose to leave home—to abandon me—I was brought to crisis point.

❀ ❀ ❀

The losses in my life were mounting up. I was having trouble sleeping, not enjoying things, feeling overwhelmed, and crying for no apparent reason.

It was Jay who made me get help. He was often better at reading my buried emotions than I was. "Darling, I know you miss Adam, but this isn't normal." He'd walked into the bedroom and found me in tears, yet again.

"How do you mean?" I blew my nose on the white handkerchief he always carried in his trouser pocket. He'd been handing me a lot of them recently.

He put an arm around my shoulders, and I stopped crying. I didn't want Jay to feel bad.

"You need to see a professional," he said.

I bristled. "I don't. In any case, I don't know where to find someone." I wasn't ready to admit I wasn't able to cope with life on my own. Yet the idea took root, and I found myself calling the psychotherapists in the yellow pages.

My first therapist, Dr. Rhein, helped me understand how losing my father as a child affected my actions. It was why I tried to control things, fearing if I didn't, everything would go terribly wrong, and I'd lose people I loved. Living that way had proved to be a spectacular mistake. Doing everything I could to ensure I was never rejected again led to my tolerating behavior I should have confronted much earlier.

One aspect of our marriage did improve. With Adam and Helenka no longer at home full-time, things between Jay and me settled down. We both worked, and he regularly traveled on business, which gave us some breathing space. I began to appreciate these separations, which made our time together less conflicted.

With no one else to look after, I could work to my own timetable, eat what I pleased, meet friends for coffee or a movie without needing to consult anyone else, and stop waiting for another shoe to drop.

Chapter 10
Susan

My sister Susan lived in London and was looking for work. With two small boys, she would only consider something part-time. In 1994, I hired her to sell advertising space for one of my clients, a magazine for American travel agents who specialized in booking Britain. She worked mostly from home, attending client meetings and the occasional trade show to provide some variety. She enjoyed it, so it was a blow to her when, a year later, she found herself more tired than she ought to be.

She put it down to being a mother to little boys—Freddie, aged six, and Bertie, three—as well as working. Her husband, John, suffered from depression and was hospitalized the following January. Shortly after, Susan was diagnosed with breast cancer, and everything she'd been trying to manage became unmanageable.

I flew to London as often as I could, accompanying her to medical appointments and helping around the house. My three other sisters and Susan's local friends did most of the heavy lifting when it came to babysitting, but I know Susan liked having me there. It wasn't altruism on my part. I had to do all I could to keep my wonderful sister alive.

* * *

Not long after her diagnosis, she came to visit and was sitting at the counter in my kitchen in Connecticut while the boys, now four and seven, played in the garden.

"Gabs." She lifted her head to look at me, ignoring the grapes I'd put in front of her as a snack. "Will you take care of Freddie and Bertie if..."

I didn't want to hear the rest of her sentence.

"Of course," I said. "But don't worry—nothing's going to happen to you."

Jay loved my sister and her family, whom he knew well by now. We'd visited them more than once in England, and Susan had come to stay with us in Fairfield several times, with the boys, including when she was ill. He wanted her to recover. Above all, he wanted me to be happy.

She last came to visit only three weeks before her death. When it became apparent she'd have to fly home earlier than planned, Jay paid for first-class tickets for Susan, her boys, and me, because first class was the only way to guarantee enough oxygen for her.

* * *

Back in the London hospital, she wasn't eating much and was sleeping a lot, though we both managed to maintain the illusion she might live. I sat at her side all day, only returning to her home late at night for a few hours' sleep before returning.

"Suzi, John's going to bring the boys to see you tomorrow."

Susan lay in the hospital, waiting for the wig seller to show her his wares. She hadn't lost much of her hair but felt she should have a wig, just in case. By now, I was sleeping on a cot in her room, not wanting her to go through this alone.

Dismay was written large on her haggard face. "I don't want to see them. I look terrible. Couldn't they come when I feel better?"

I could have told her they needed to see her because they missed her and couldn't wait for her to come home. That wasn't the reason. Though I'd never uttered the thought, I knew this would be their final chance to be with her.

"I think they ought to come," I said.

Susan's eyes met mine. I think we were both remembering the last time we'd seen Daddy. He was in Archway Hospital, miles away from where we lived, and the long trip on the London Tube had been something of an adventure at the time. He'd died a few days later.

"Gabs, am I dying?" she asked.

So here we were. The knowledge I'd been trying to suppress, as I accompanied her to interviews with the surgeon, through her chemo, to the recent draining of fluid in her lungs, had risen to the surface at last.

"I don't think you've got as long as we thought," I was making a herculean effort to keep my voice steady. I could feel tears pricking the backs of my eyelids.

"They're too young for me to leave them," she whispered. "They'll forget me."

"I won't let them," I promised. Even so, I felt caught off-guard when she died.

❖ ❖ ❖

When the chips were down, I could rely on Jay to do the right thing, and now I was thankful. His mother had died only days after Susan, and he told me he felt like an orphan too. Perhaps that was part of the reason he immediately agreed to give Fred and Bertie a home, if their dad was okay with it.

Many men, aged sixty, faced with having two small boys to take care of, might have balked. But my good-hearted husband flew to London for a couple of days, specifically to talk this over with John, who seemed almost relieved when he knew they'd be loved and cared for by us.

So, Jay and I brought the boys to America. The whirlwind of activity resulting from that decision—getting them passports and visas, packing and shipping their things, not to mention endeavoring to make sure they had comfort and reassurance—helped stave off the grief following Susan's death.

It had been almost twenty years since my kids were that age. A relative truce had been established between our four children and us. Still, despite their being adults now, they, too, had to get used to the idea they were no longer the only children in our lives.

Meanwhile, I had underestimated the difficulties of becoming a mother again. My time was suddenly divided, and Jay, who'd become accustomed to being one of a couple, found himself one of a foursome again. He asked me, more than once, to get a live-in nanny, but I didn't want another permanent member of the household.

I believed these boys needed my attention, not that of a stranger who knew nothing about their mother or their life in Britain. Besides, I needed them, too—they were a link to the sister I'd lost. After a few months, finding I couldn't manage everything, I hired part-time help, but even this wasn't enough to enable me to run my company, so I gave it up.

I tried to be as much like a mother to them as I could without attempting to replace Susan. Being an aunt kept me one step removed from motherhood, which made it easier to give them a little space.

The boys were apt to resent me at first, simply because I wasn't their mother. They were scrupulous about correcting anyone who made that mistake, and I understood.

Jay and I did morph, eventually, into "parental units," and then after a decade and a half into "my folks," or in my case, to "my mom." That's the American m-o-m, pronounced in an authentic Connecticut accent, not the English "Mummy" of their early childhood. They never called me Mom directly—always Gabi or Gab, which felt more comfortable for all of us. Jay was always Jay.

As things turned out, they never went back to live in England, though they visited their father every year. He stayed in contact with them, sending them regular letters, books, and toys he thought they might like. When they visited, he made a superhuman effort to be a father to them, but would often relapse into depression after they left. Five years after they first arrived, with his consent, we adopted them.

Chapter 11
More Problems

Living with someone who has a close relationship with alcohol is a tricky business. Liquor affects everyone differently—both the drinker and the people around him. Unaccustomed to drinking very much, a large glass of sauvignon blanc, or one gin and tonic, if strong enough, was apt to make me feel relaxed and sometimes even giggly. I never liked feeling out of control of my behavior, so I generally stopped at that.

Jay used to laugh at my lack of tolerance for it. "You're such a cheap date," he'd tease me.

Since Jay was taller and heavier than me, he could probably consume more, but I was amazed at the amount he put away without any apparent side effects. Over dinner with friends, I noticed he would manage to drink at least one more glass of wine than everyone else, often two or three.

It was doing me no good to count the glasses – it simply made me more distressed.

I had no concept of what an alcoholic really was, despite having been married to Robin. We were so young then, and many of our friends sometimes drank too much, as young people do.

When I imagined alcoholics, if I pictured them at all, I thought of *The Rake's Progress*, or the destroyed lives of men lying in the gutters of the Bowery. I pictured people imbibing methylated spirits and mouthwash out of desperation, and hiding bottles of liquor around the house.

I think Jay thought of drunks that way, too. So, he could never relate alcoholism to a functional corporate executive like him. The three-martini lunch was a cliché in the Madison Avenue world of the 1960s when he worked in the advertising department of *Reader's Digest,* and taking clients out for long boozy lunches was the norm.

Like many "hidden" alcoholics, Jay was so functional that it seemed incredible something as transparent as vodka could be endangering our marriage. Like most out-of-control drinkers, he just didn't, or wouldn't, see it.

He never became what many would consider drunk; he never slurred his words, rarely lost his balance, and never became aggressive. So, if there was a glassy, unfocused look to his eye, it was gone the next day. Yet I couldn't explain the feeling that things weren't right, somehow. After all, he never missed a day's work, and only had the rare fender-bender, unlike some of the other horror stories I'd heard.

But somewhere, deep down, I was aware something was off, even before I married him.

❊ ❊ ❊

When we first met in Copenhagen, one of my co-workers commented that Jay was a man trying to preserve himself for posterity by pickling himself in vodka. It strikes me now I wouldn't have remembered that throwaway remark if it hadn't struck a chord.

Before we were to marry, Jay took me for a romantic weekend tryst in the country. After a few drinks, though, he fell asleep on the hearthrug in front of the fireplace, and I spent the evening alone, watching him and silently seething at the loss of this precious time with each other.

I wanted to be understanding. If anything was driving Jay to drink, I told myself, it was the divorce from his first wife, which was still painful for him. She was distressed, and he felt guilty. Once we were together permanently, he would reduce his intake, I was sure.

Not long after we married, though, I started to worry in earnest about my husband's other romance—the one with alcohol. I had no understanding of the way this affected me. I began to refuse an evening gin and tonic, hoping he'd pass on his cocktail. He didn't. Or couldn't.

I found it hard to put my finger on why Jay's drinking bothered me so much. Before his first drink of the day, he was still the interesting and interested man I'd fallen in love with and married. After trying evenings, my loving feelings would resurface in the morning, and life would go on.

He was always affectionate, willing to comfort me if I felt sad, waking for a snuggle before he went to work, coming up behind me to hug me as I stood in the kitchen making dinner.

He was generous, even when sometimes his expenditures made me nervous. He paid for both his daughters' college education at private colleges and Helenka's boarding school. Later he paid for Freddie and Bertie to go to university.

He encouraged my success at work and talked me through my failures.

"That client doesn't deserve someone like you," he'd say, if I lost a bid to represent a hotel or tour operator. "If they can't see how great you are, it's their loss."

And he made our bed every day before breakfast.

"That will be my job," he announced before we married. We were doing this mundane task together, straightening the pillows and the wedding ring patterned patchwork quilt I'd found at a flea market near Chicago.

I looked up and patted the mattress. "That's wonderful." I was eager to encourage any contribution to the house-work. We wouldn't be able to afford anyone to help, and riding herd on my kids resulted in only limited success.

Jay went out a few days later and bought a duvet. So, each morning, for the duration of our marriage, with a deft flick of his wrist, the bed was made. He helped with some other chores, but on the whole, preferred to leave them to me. When we finally did have a little more money, he insisted I hire someone. He wanted me to have less to do, since I was working and looking after the two little boys who'd joined our family.

In spite of all the positive things, I came to realize his alcohol consumption kept raising an emotional barrier between us. Most evenings, he couldn't keep track of a conversation or the plot of a movie we were watching.

I refused to let him drive home after evenings out. To begin with, he insisted he was fine, but when I refused to get into the car as a passenger, I think he realized that he might be better off, too, if I became his chauffeur.

Only I appeared to notice these patterns of behavior, and I retreated emotionally to protect my heart.

I began to suffer from depression and couldn't understand why. Jay, oblivious to much of the world around him, always knew what I was feeling, at least until the first drink of the day. His being in tune with my feelings was one of the reasons I loved him. But I didn't want to hear what he was saying now.

"I'm not the one with the problem," he said. "I think you're depressed. You should see someone."

No wonder he needed a drink, I thought, with a depressed wife. I found a therapist who told me I was suffering from the chronic depression and anxiety common to people who'd lost a parent in childhood. I wondered if I was scared of losing Jay to alcohol. So, I did the therapy and took the anti-depressants, which helped. Yet the booze remained a barrier unless everything else was going well.

My friend Debra referred to it as the "frog-in-the-pot syndrome." If you throw a frog into boiling water, it will jump right out to save itself. If you place it into cold water and then slowly turn the heat up, it won't realize it's being cooked until it's too late. I felt like the frog.

It wasn't as though any of this was intentional. I don't think Jay wanted to push me away. He just wanted me to let him drink whenever and whatever he liked.

No one else in the family commented that Jay wasn't too sharp by bedtime. He tuned out, and his hearing became less acute. I began to feel lonely, even though he was sitting in the same room.

When he started passing out in front of the television at night, he called it falling asleep and put it down to hard work and fatigue.

At first, I took him at face value and would patiently wake him and encourage him up to bed. I'm not sure he even wondered how he'd made it to our bedroom. As time went on, I would leave him to make his own way upstairs, where I'd be asleep or pretending to be. He began to notice when I left him to sleep it off downstairs.

"Why didn't you wake me?" he would say, aggrieved.

"I knew you'd come upstairs eventually." I kept my voice neutral, and he realized that I wouldn't change my mind.

I started to notice a pattern in his daily routine. He'd go to the office late, often leaving the house at eight-thirty or nine, and returning at eight in the evening. He could do this because he was the company president and insisted it was logical, since he got more work done after people had gone home. Besides, he said, he hated the drive to and from the office in rush-hour traffic.

When he did arrive home, he'd mix himself a martini and go upstairs to change.

"I need to unwind," he'd say. "It's been a tough day."

This made sense, of course, as did the long hours. What I'd forgotten was that he often spent lunch hours in his favorite Italian greasy spoon, where martinis were on the menu. He also had a drinks cabinet next to his desk and would always have a martini to hand as he worked late. He never made a secret of this. Every CEO had alcohol for visitors, he claimed. I had no idea if that was true.

Once home, he might follow his first with another—a "little dividend"—plus two or three glasses of wine with dinner, and even, in the early days, a nightcap of brandy. He'd pop a Tylenol before going to sleep and leap out of bed the next morning without any symptoms of a hangover.

At work, his employees overlooked their boss's alcoholism, not just because he was a success, but because in every other way, he was a wonderful man as well as a great boss and colleague. When he retired at the age of sixty-seven, the office organized a party for him.

Many of his employees and colleagues shared anecdotes at the event, showing how much they loved him and how grateful they were for his leadership, mentorship, and loyalty. Almost every story included a reference, usually affectionate, to his drinking. It was so much a part of his identity that it seemed natural to them to include it.

But for me, alcohol was the choice Jay repeatedly made instead of choosing me.

Al-Anon advocated detachment with love, and I did still love him. All too often, though, I was only detaching when my anger forced me to do so. Jay knew this, but he was as stubborn as I was and wouldn't give an inch. I didn't know what to do as the amount he consumed kept increasing. I loved him, but I wanted him to stop drinking. He loved me but didn't want to, or couldn't, quit. Impasse.

Neither of us noticed the cracks in our relationship insidiously turning into fissures.

How much of it all was my fault? I spent a lot of time

wondering about that over the years. The cliché *she drove him to drink*, I reasoned, existed because it was true. Jay never blamed me for his dependency. On the other hand, he would tell me I was the only one concerned about his intake, which proved there was nothing wrong with him. I started to doubt myself, and it was years before other people in the family began to acknowledge that his drinking worried them, too.

I found our conflicting views of the situation more and more intolerable, though I felt I should take responsibility for some of it. As I was to learn subsequently, this feeling that I was to blame is not uncommon in people living with a problem drinker.

My friends in Al-Anon suggested I focus on myself, pointing out that I could do nothing until my spouse hit bottom and his life became unmanageable. Jay seemed to have no bottom. Over the years, he rode out every obstacle with a confidence that was no doubt helped along by his favorite tipple.

He did quit drinking more than once. He insisted he could stop, as he had with smoking, but only when he was away from home. He considered it just a habit, and breaking his daily routine would make it easier.

He wasn't dependent on booze and could stop drinking any time, he said. Anyone married to an alcoholic will know this is something most of them believe. From Al-Anon, though, I'd learned that Jay was the only one who could decide when he would give it up, and all I could do was to stand by and hope.

So, I kept going to the Al-Anon meetings. Jay kept drinking.

He gave up several times over the years. Each time he did, it was while he was away from his day-to-day routine, and he managed it cold turkey, with no visible withdrawal symptoms. He was irritable for a while, but he'd always had a temper, so I couldn't say it had anything to do with his getting sober.

The first time he decided to reduce his intake was a few months after we married. He began by giving it up at lunch.

"If it doesn't work, I'll give it up totally," he vowed.

His method failed, and two years passed before he tried to quit again.

That time, he stayed on the wagon for almost a year, and then he picked up a glass again.

✳ ✳ ✳

His periods of sobriety were wonderful, to begin with. I was more affectionate, trusting that now I was dealing with the real Jay. We talked about our issues and listened to each other. After some months, though, he would turn to alcohol again.

"You see?" he'd say. "I've proved I'm not an alcoholic—I can quit any time."

It sounded almost logical.

I proposed he try Alcoholics Anonymous more than once, and he went to a few meetings before announcing he wasn't like the rest of the members. Their stories were so dire, Jay said. He couldn't identify with tales of drunken parties, blackouts, car crashes, failed relationships, and lost jobs. We lived in an upscale suburb, so I felt sure there were high-functioning alcoholics like him in the program, but he was looking for an excuse not to go, and he found one.

My going to Al-Anon meetings in the evening made the situation noticeably more tense. In Jay's mind, every meeting I went to, leaving him at home, was a deliberate provocation. I tried to avoid getting his back up—Al-Anon called it treading on eggshells. To stave off his irritation, I switched to morning meetings and would sneak out of the house at seven a.m.

One evening, he mixed himself a martini with a couple

of small white pickled onions. "You're addicted to those meetings," he remarked, conversationally, before taking a sip.

I felt a rush of guilt. He might be right. I found it difficult to face the day without a meeting where I could offload my preoccupation with my husband's drinking.

"I wouldn't need to go if you didn't drink." I could hear my own irritation and defensiveness, though I forced myself to stay calm. A conversation begun after six in the evening would never resolve anything.

"I'm not the one with the problem," he said. "People have been drinking cocktails before dinner for years."

I tried a lighter approach. "Oh, that's so old-fashioned. Nobody does that anymore."

In point of fact, the eighties had seen an upsurge in cocktail culture, but it wasn't quite the same as the methodical downing of martinis, which was the norm in the media world of the sixties when Jay's career began.

Jay wasn't to be sidetracked by arguments like these.

"My parents drank cocktails and aperitifs all their lives, and it never hurt them."

"Maybe not," I conceded. Meanwhile, I wondered what it had done to his family relationships. His relatives never got together without liquor playing a major part. Hors d'oeuvres would take forever to consume to allow more time for an aperitif or two. Jay argued that his private cocktail hour was just something he liked, not an addiction. It sounded plausible, but I wasn't so sure.

"Anyway, if I'm an alcoholic, you're obese."

He knew this was a low blow because I struggled to keep my weight down. It was true I tended to eat in a haphazard way and was apt to comfort myself with food when I was unhappy. My weight fluctuated over the years, but I was always within ten to twenty pounds of where I'd been at eighteen. I'd tried every known diet, and most of them had worked for a while, then stopped working, once

I thought I'd gotten my eating under control again.

"At least I *try* to watch what I eat," I shot back. "You won't even attempt to cut down."

"I'm an all-or-nothing guy," he would say. That was true, too.

As I kept hoping Jay would stop drinking, I continued to read books, searching for solutions. The 1980s and '90s were boom years for books that aimed to sort out one's problems, and sometimes I felt I was keeping those authors going singlehandedly. I hoped each one would have the answer. Most suggested communication was a key element in successful relationships. Our problem was that after a drink or two, Jay was difficult to communicate with. I had no idea how to reach him, to explain how much I missed the man I'd fallen in love with.

Chapter 12
New Hampshire

In August 1990, Jay decided to quit drinking for good. This time he meant it, he insisted. He was not going to drink again, and the best way to do it would be to leave town for a week, out of temptation's way. In the first flush of delight at this development, and despite previous disappointments, I agreed to go camping with him.

I wasn't much of a camper. Frankly, as I joked to anyone who'd listen, sleeping in any hostelry where they didn't put a chocolate on my pillow counted as camping to me. Still, I was game to make the effort. So, I accompanied Jay on weekends at state parks and campgrounds without too much complaining. I became accustomed to the taste of burned bacon and weak tea—the water never seemed to boil. But I never got used to the mosquitoes, always in abundant supply, no matter what else might be lacking.

Delighted that I'd agreed so willingly to this proposal, Jay suggested we go further afield than usual. He booked a spot in a campsite near Keene in southern New Hampshire. For the first two days, I only had to rise above minor inconveniences. On the third day, it started to rain and didn't stop.

The chief camper was delighted. The sound of raindrops on the tent above our heads reminded him of his Minnesota vacations as a child, in a log cabin with a tin roof. The same noise reminded me of my first ever night under canvas.

My parents, four sisters, and I, vacationing in Europe, were crammed into a huge army surplus tent in Belgium when it began to pour. Soon water was running through the canvas and down the inside of the tent roof. We had pitched it directly on the ground, without a tarpaulin, and the water was making its way in. Even my parents, war veterans used to roughing it, had trouble looking cheerful.

Back in New Hampshire, I wondered what we might do that day without getting wet.

"I know," suggested Jay. "Let's go and look at houses."

I must have looked startled.

"For a weekend place," he explained.

I never wanted a weekend place, being a person who liked to vary my vacation spots by traveling somewhere different each year. On the other hand, I love looking at other people's homes, so I agreed.

A bespectacled Realtor, fiftyish and wearing a bright floral dress that made her resemble an armchair, worked from an office in the front room of her saltbox-style house. I noticed a faint smell of damp as she welcomed us in, but it might have been us. She'd be delighted to show us the area, she smiled, as she grabbed a raincoat and a fishing hat from the hooks by the door. Soon we were being shown the local attractions, some of them, like the top of Mount Monadnock, hard to make out in the drizzle.

"Have you got anything on the water?" asked Jay. "A lake would be nice." At that moment, the car plowed through a large puddle at the side of the road, causing a tiny tidal wave.

The houses were depressing. The more the Realtor pointed out how full of potential a cottage was, the more I noticed the sagging cabinets, the uneven floors, or the damp stain, partially hidden behind a strategically placed armoire.

"I don't think so," Jay decided as we drove back to her house.

She ran a hand through her salt-and-pepper hair.

"I know what you want." She ushered us into a couple of chairs in her office, where we dripped quietly onto the carpet.

"You want New London."

"Really? Where's that?"

"It's about two hours north, right on Lake Sunapee. I know a Realtor there." She began to rummage through the flyers that cascaded across her desk.

"Aha." She fished out a business card from beneath a pile of local maps. "Here he is—Dave Buxton. I'll call him right now."

❖ ❖ ❖

It continued to rain as I struggled to get comfortable on the air mattress that night. I avoided liquids so I wouldn't have to leave the tent in the middle of the night, but even so, I was a very damp camper by the time the next morning rolled around.

Dave had organized visits to five different properties in New London. I had to admit, as we drove around in his Range Rover, that, even in the rain, the place was pretty, with its white clapboard houses, town green, and small liberal arts college. The surrounding scenery was gorgeous, with a couple of mountains disappearing into the mist and pastoral farmland and lakes enough to satisfy Jay.

"See, darling? It's a picture-perfect small New England town."

"It is," confirmed Dave. "There's only three thousand full-time residents, and we like it that way."

"I like that there's a college." I thought of the students

who would bring a younger vibe to the place for at least half the year.

"You're right, Gabi—we're near sailing and skiing and mountain hiking, too."

I could see by my spouse's expression he was looking forward to equipping himself for all these new sports. And yet. None of the houses we saw was quite what he claimed to be looking for.

"We don't want a condo, or a Swiss chalet, or a farmhouse off the beaten track," he said, naming some of the places we'd been shown. "Do you have anything on the water?"

"And your budget?" murmured Dave.

Jay heard him. "Don't let's worry about that now."

I certainly wasn't worried about the budget. We weren't really going to buy a house. We were just staying out of the wet.

The last house of the day was a tiny wooden cottage on a pond not far from the middle of town. A steep driveway ended in a small parking area, where the selling agent, introduced as Pam, was waiting, looking hopeful. It was an odd house, bigger than it appeared.

We entered to find a bedroom and the bathroom on either side of the front door. Steps led down to the living room with its cathedral ceiling and small open-plan kitchen. We found another small room, with two single beds squeezed into it, off the main one. Three sets of sliding glass doors opened onto a deck that ran around the house. Even so, the interior was a bit gloomy in this weather.

"You could sit out here and enjoy the scenery," said Dave, shivering slightly beneath his umbrella. It was an attractive view, to be sure, at least it might be when the mist disappeared. Right now, I was glad to be inside, looking out at the rain. At the bottom of the stairs stood a black wood-burning stove, which gave the promise of heat on a cold day. Pam caught me looking at it. "It heats the whole place."

She indicated the long metal chimney that disappeared into the roof. "Saves on electricity."

"I could put the barbecue here, sweetheart," yelled Jay from outside. I didn't like the sound of this. Surely, he was only saying it to encourage the Realtors? He walked back inside.

"Perhaps you'd like a minute?" Dave was looking over my head at Pam, standing behind me. Was that a gleam in his eye?

Jay waited until they were out of earshot. "We could afford this, darling." He grinned.

"But..." We weren't going to buy it, were we?

"It's the right size, on a lake..."

"Pond," I interrupted.

"Practically new..."

"Twelve years old," I said.

"Plus, it's ready to move into," he finished. He was a better salesman than the real-estate agents. I tried, unsuccessfully, to think of something else to stem this torrent of enthusiasm.

"Tell you what," he went on. "Why don't we stay over until tomorrow and look at it again when things dry out."

"Stay over?" The idea was tempting.

"Sure."

"You mean in an actual hotel with an actual bed?" I hadn't been looking forward to driving back to our soggy tent. "Done."

We had an elegant dinner in the two-hundred-year-old New London Inn, and Jay sent the wine waiter away. I gazed at him, sober and happy, with new hope. After all, he'd given up drinking. It had been almost a week now. Perhaps he deserved a reward. Not a house, though.

The inn had no rooms available, so we ended up in the Lantern Motel. Our room, decorated, I guessed, some years before, in brown and beige, had little furniture—but it did have a real bed.

I woke up the next morning to find the sun streaming through a chink in the curtains. Oh, dear. Jay would be so disappointed when I said no to the purchase.

I chickened out. Two hours later, in brilliant sunshine, we bought the house.

A couple of months later, having proved to his own satisfaction that he wasn't an alcoholic, Jay began drinking again.

* * *

Weekends in New Hampshire highlighted the progress of his alcohol dependency. We'd leave on Fridays and come back on Sunday, as so many people do. The worst time to set off was always between four and six in the afternoon when the traffic was at its height. So, we'd become accustomed, when I was my own boss, to leaving at around three, which suited Jay.

When the boys came to live with us, this no longer worked so well. At first, my husband would drive us up, so we'd leave after they finished school. We'd stop about halfway, in Massachusetts, and have something to eat at a restaurant. Jay would have a drink or two, and dinner took time. Freddie and Bertie, being young, would be tired out by the time we arrived in New London.

I suggested we simply head to McDonald's, get something for the boys, and carry on to New Hampshire, so we'd be there by eight or so, with plenty of time to eat dinner.

It was only a matter of weeks before Jay began to be irritable on the second leg of the journey.

One Friday, he came back from the half-day in the office and went straight to the bedroom. I followed him.

"This just isn't working," he announced. "I need to get up there earlier."

I was puzzled.

"I have to get the mail, and the post office closes at six." He avoided my eye as he threw some clean underwear and socks into the hold-all he used for weekends in the country.

We did have a mailbox in New London, and we could easily have collected our letters on Saturday morning, but it soon dawned on me that wasn't the point. The point was, he needed a drink around six o'clock each day, and McDonald's didn't solve that problem.

I wasn't going to rush so that Jay could have a drink, so I told him I'd drive up separately whenever the boys and I were ready. I wasn't aware that this was another of those small cracks that would eventually get wider.

Chapter 13
Intervention

Jay sold his company in 2001 and used some of the money to buy a piece of land on Lake Sunapee, not far from the weekend cottage we already had in New Hampshire. He could afford it now, and he felt he deserved it. I couldn't argue with that. He'd given his all to make the business a success.

It was a lovely piece of land, one we made even more attractive over the years. Every room had a view of the water, and looking out, one could see the stone deck, bordered with giant boulders, some of which had been found when the foundations were excavated.

We planted the edge of the terrace with small yellow daylilies and miniature iris. Below it was the lawn and beyond that, stretching to the shore, was the wild part of the garden, where Japanese primula, crimson lobelia, and celandine jostled for attention among the ferns and jewelweed. At six feet tall, Joe Pye-weed towered over the rest all summer. Beyond lay the lake, anchored by the half-dozen pines whose lower branches Jay had trimmed to improve the view.

But the house never felt like ours—it was always Jay's.

Eventually, he told me he was building this place intending to make no-income-tax New Hampshire our legal residence.

I told myself we'd only have to be there for six months and a day each year to qualify as residents, and if so, Jay was easily fulfilling that requirement. I never fully realized that he intended it to be our permanent full-time home. I believed we were replacing our two-bedroom cottage with a larger-than-life second home, where we would enjoy weekends, vacations, and holidays with friends and family.

To begin with, that's what we did. Since our social life in Connecticut was now non-existent, we would invite friends up for the weekend. If they invited us to their homes in Connecticut, we were never available because we were at the lake. This kept our circle of friends small, since our current friends had no chance to introduce us to new ones. Eventually, they stopped inviting us.

Jay spent most weekdays in Connecticut, working as a consultant for the company he'd just sold. Gradually, he began to spend more and more time at the lake house, and as time passed, he made it his primary home.

I never wanted to live there full time—we still owned a home in the posh part of Fairfield. Although the new property was bigger and more luxurious, I would never have chosen something so large to look after. Jay was the moving force behind it, having bought the land, hired the builders, and supervised the construction.

I would accompany him when he had meetings with the architects, mainly to make sure the house he built would be easy to manage. I suggested putting the master bedroom on the ground floor, and chose lever door handles to make opening them easier for older hands. Still, I worried it was much too substantial for a weekend place. Or for a full-time home for just two people.

New Hampshire was beautiful, a wonderful place to relax, and the little town of New London was as picturesque as one might wish. I enjoyed being there when I felt like getting away from my day-to-day life. I grew up in the real London, in England, and in New Hampshire, I felt the lack of my writing community and the stimulating cultural life of Connecticut.

Jay was content to enjoy the house he'd built and play a little golf. He liked having our family and old friends visit, and taking them by boat across the lake to the small harbor with the summer restaurant. It was like being on vacation, and vacations were good. I just couldn't do it year-round.

Jay always claimed he would spend his money before he died, and, after he sold his company, he spent quite a bit of it on exotic journeys around the world. A friend of ours, married to one of Jay's Yale classmates, was a travel agent, and put together groups of around eight to ten friends who traveled to such places as Vietnam, New Zealand, and Europe. We'd taken some wonderful trips together.

Having people around took some of the strain off Jay's and my relationship. They'd known him since his college days and made allowances if they saw him the worse for wear. I had other travelers to talk to as we visited old temples in Asia, hot chocolate shops in Bratislava, or wilderness lodges Down Under.

I fretted about the cost for a while but concluded that, since I had no influence over him, I would make the most of these spectacular adventures. I was glad we went, since these experiences provided a trove of irreplaceable memories to be savored years later.

When we weren't traveling or hosting guests, I preferred to be in Fairfield, while Jay only felt at home in New Hampshire. We might not have reached this stalemate if, over the years, we'd managed to talk and reached a compromise about how much time we spent together.

I soon realized that taking care of two houses was both time-consuming and expensive, and suggested we sell our Fairfield house and buy a smaller one downtown. This, I hinted, would serve as a pied-à-terre whenever Jay needed to be in New York. He agreed, though I think he had some doubts about allowing me even this toehold in Connecticut.

For ten years, I did my best to divide my time between our cottage in Fairfield and the lake house, but Jay never felt it was enough. Generally, I managed four days by the lake and three in Connecticut, but he resented the time I spent away from him, while I began to grudge every visit to New Hampshire. As the drip, drip, drip of his drinking put an ever-greater distance between us, I felt lonelier with him than I felt by myself.

* * *

By 2012, not only I, but other members of the family, were being adversely affected by Jay's drinking. Amanda and her wife, Barb, had told me they wouldn't be visiting New Hampshire as often because they didn't want their children exposed to it. Heather worried about her father and sympathized with my distress, but continued to drive up, albeit not so often.

Adam and Helenka saw less of him than the others did. After their alcoholic father, Robin, died of diabetes because he'd been unable to give up booze, they were all too aware of the possible consequences of alcoholism.

Fred, now twenty-four, was living at Sunset Shores, the New Hampshire lake house, at the time, and was one of the most impacted since he was with Jay every day. Less crucial issues, like the lack of focus after a few drinks, were difficult enough to accept. But he began to have blackouts, a classic symptom of alcoholism, where he didn't remember anything he'd said or done the night before.

When Jay fell a couple of times and I wasn't around, Fred became distressed and angry at having to take responsibility for him.

Bertie, our youngest, was the child who was least involved with the family, which he explained by saying we were all crazy. He never admitted he was avoiding us deliberately, but after graduating from college he didn't come to see us very often, though he lived only an hour and a half away.

I was never the sort of mother to insist on a child's presence if they weren't willing. I kept my expectations low and preferred infrequent visits from someone who wanted to see me, rather than lots of them out of a sense of duty. My husband, though, expected more.

Finally, things came to a head. Jay and I were having yet another pointless discussion about his quitting drinking, or at least cutting down. He was in the kitchen making his second martini of the evening.

"You're the only person who thinks I drink too much," he remarked, not for the first time. "You imagine everyone's a drunk."

It was true that I tended to notice problem drinkers when we ran across them, since I'd heard so many descriptions of the symptoms in Al-Anon meetings. On this occasion, though, I decided to throw caution to the winds.

"Your daughters both agree," I said. "They've told me so."

There was a moment's heavy silence before he turned to glare at me.

"You've been talking about this with Amanda and Heather?"

I realized I'd hit a nerve, and anything that followed would be a waste of time. Discussing him with his daughters constituted a breach of confidence in his eyes—to me, remaining silent was just a way of keeping secrets, and damaging ones, at that.

I plowed on. Might as well be hung for a sheep...

"I didn't bring the subject up. They've both independently said they're worried about you."

"Well, you can tell them there's no need to worry. I know what I'm doing, and I don't need any suggestions from you." He paused and then added: "While we're on the topic, when are you going to lose a few pounds?"

As always, this signaled the end of the conversation because I would no longer rise to the bait. These days, I was able to ignore this kind of jibe. He only brought this subject up when there was nothing else he could say.

❅ ❅ ❅

It occurred to me that if I could get all the members of the family to explain to Jay how anxious they were, he might begin to believe we needed him to stop. I'd heard about interventions and speculated as to whether we could attempt something like that.

There was a logistical issue, of course. It was rare for all of us to be in New Hampshire simultaneously. Because there wasn't room for all the family to stay at the same time, we tended to stagger visits. That summer, Freddie and Bertie were there, working at the golf course to earn some money.

Amanda, Barb, and their children were staying at a friend's house on the other side of the lake. Adam, his bipolar disorder under control for the time being, was living in Vermont with his girlfriend, helping her with her construction business. He agreed to drive up if we decided to go ahead. Heather and Helenka were at home in Connecticut and likely relieved they wouldn't have to deal with a confrontation.

In an intervention, the presence of a professional moderator is recommended, but to find someone in New Hampshire who'd be prepared to come on a Sunday afternoon proved impossible. It was also customary to have a bed pre-reserved at some sort of rehab, so a drinker could be hospitalized before he or she had a chance to change their mind. I didn't do that. Ambushing Jay was likely to be tough enough without trying to force him into a facility the same day.

My therapist put me in touch with an intervention specialist, Mr. Sobieski, in Fairfield, so I called him to ask for help.

"I know I can't do this the traditional way," I explained, "but I wondered if you could give me some pointers, given the situation."

He thought for a minute.

"Well, it's rather unorthodox. I don't normally recommend people do this without professional support."

"I understand that, but I don't think I've got a choice right now. I have to do something, and next weekend is the only time I can get enough of the family together."

"Tell me what your goals are," he said. "What are you hoping to achieve?"

I had a ready answer for him. I'd been thinking about this for some time.

"Well, of course, I want him to get help. I'm almost certain he won't go to AA, and it's a hundred percent definite he won't want to go to rehab."

As I talked, it occurred to me this might not work at all. Jay had only to refuse to concede there was a problem, and the effort would fail. I forced myself to listen as Mr. Sobieski asked me some more questions.

"Do you think you might persuade him to do a four-day drying-out spell? There's an addiction recovery program at Greenwich Hospital, which is quite intensive and has outpatient follow-up. It's full of important people who can't afford to take time off work."

Was that a hint of irony in his voice? No matter.

This sounded fine to me. I liked this man. He wasn't too intimidating, and he obviously understood the alcoholic brain.

"I'll call you on Monday and let you know what happens," I said. "If it's been successful, I'll be sure to make an appointment."

* * *

Yet another gorgeous day in late summer found the family preparing to gather on the terrace. Fred and Bertie sat, jaws clenched with nerves, which was only natural. They were risking Jay's negative response, something none of our children wanted. The day before, I had driven around the lake to where Amanda was staying to ask her to participate in the intervention. Her wife, Barb, was a pastoral counselor, so she was familiar with the pros and cons, and I thought she might be able to advise her spouse.

"This doesn't feel right." I could hear the doubt in Amanda's voice. "I need more time."

I hadn't anticipated this. She'd made it clear that her dad's drinking bothered her. Confronting him about it was another matter.

"I know it's short notice, but these are the only dates when I have at least some of you here. I think things will only get worse if we don't do something as soon as we can."

I had the sense Amanda was unhappy about being put on the spot like this, but after giving it some thought, she agreed to show up the next morning.

I was on edge as I waited for the sound of her car in the driveway. Had she changed her mind? This had no hope of working without her. Hearing from the boys and me wouldn't be enough to convince Jay. He might argue that I'd influenced them.

Amanda was his daughter, and what she thought about this mattered. After all, concern about the influence of Jay's drinking on their children was why they weren't staying at our house. I stopped pacing as I heard her arrive. She walked into the house without knocking, as all the kids did.

"Hi, Dad," She gave him a peck on the cheek.

"To what do we owe the pleasure?" he asked with a smile.

"Oh, I thought I'd come and see you." A slight tremor in Amanda's voice betrayed her anxiety, but if Jay heard it, he didn't comment.

"How about some coffee?" I offered. "I'll bring it outside if you like."

She was particular about her coffee, and I was sure I wouldn't make it the way she liked it, so I felt relieved when she chose water.

"Coming right up." I watched the two of them walk out of the house and went to find Adam and the boys.

"I guess we can begin," I told them.

I wanted to say my piece perfectly, so I'd written out my thoughts on five small white index cards. I took a breath. "Jayway." Jayway was the nickname only I was allowed to use.

He glanced up, surprised to see so many of us crowding onto the terrace. "We want to talk to you."

"Sounds serious."

"It is, I guess." I took the cards out of the back pocket of my shorts and sat down. "What I—we—have to say is important. I've written some of it down, so I don't forget anything."

An uneasy expression crossed Jay's face and he shifted slightly on the Adirondack chair.

"First, I need you to know that I love you. You're the love of my life." I had to make this clear. I glanced at card one. "I respect your choices, and I know I can't make you do anything you don't want to do."

"Is this about my drinking?"

I nodded. "I have to say what I need to, so I'm going to keep going, okay?"

My husband gave an unconvincing nod.

"I think I'm speaking for all of us when I say I'm concerned about the effects of alcohol on your health and abilities." Jay's eyebrows shot up in surprise. I could see he wanted to reply, but I carried on without giving him a chance to speak.

"You've had these falls recently, which has been hard on Fred. He's had to pick you up a couple of times. I know you say you fainted, but even if that's true, it shows something's wrong."

Jay remained silent. I glanced down at the next card.

"Your temper is getting worse, which is difficult for us to deal with. You're finding it hard to follow the plot of a movie after six in the evening. We have to keep pausing the video to explain it to you."

I couldn't see his face now. He was staring at the ground. I needed to get to the way this made me feel.

"I'm sad, darling. I miss the man I married. You're here, but you're slipping away."

He was betraying no clue as to his reaction. Well, I had nothing to lose now, so I might as well continue.

"I love you, but you know I hate the liquor. I want something better for us."

Jay lifted his head a few inches. Not much of a response, but I took it as a sign he was paying attention.

"I want to look forward to doing things with you, not wait for you to do some damage to yourself."

The children sat, completely silent, watching him.

After a moment, he spoke. "You all feel this way?"

They looked at each other and murmured their agreement.

"I think you should hear from them directly," I clarified. "They love you and want you to get better."

One by one they described the effect his deteriorating health and behavior had on them. Fred confirmed that he worried about Jay's falls. He felt anxious anticipating the next fall or accident. Jay had run his speedboat aground on a rock recently, and broken his knee when he crashed the snowmobile he'd bought.

If he were at home, Fred continued, it would be his responsibility, and if he were out, Jay might not get help.

Bertie explained that he didn't bring girlfriends home any more because he worried that Jay might do something embarrassing when he was drinking. Jay claimed he was teasing someone Bertie had invited, but they found his questions intrusive and impossible to answer.

Amanda confirmed she was bringing the children to stay less frequently, because she and Barb didn't think Jay was a good example for them, after he'd had a couple of drinks. They wouldn't let the kids go in the boat with him anymore, at least not after he'd had a drink, because his driving worried them.

Adam, always extremely forgiving, since he'd been forgiven many times for his conduct when he was having a manic bipolar episode, mostly nodded and told Jay that he thought he could do anything he set his mind to.

Jay listened and even smiled encouragingly now and again. This was going so much better than I'd dared to hope. I think the kids felt it too, and it gave them the confidence to have their say. They were great. It took a lot of courage to sit down and tell the man they loved he needed to change. When they'd finished, I raised my head.

"So, what do you think? You can see we're all anxious about this. We love you and always want you to be head of the family." I could see Jay was happy to hear this. "Perhaps if you could do this for yourself as well as for us, things will get better."

"I hear you." A beat. "But I'm not a drunk."

My stomach began to churn.

"I can give up any time." So here we were again. The same old argument.

"Anyway," he sighed. "I can see this means a lot to you, so I will stop."

Thank God.

"However." Oh, no. My shoulders tensed up again. I was beginning to perspire in the heat and wondered if I'd put on sunblock that morning. I made myself concentrate on what he was saying.

"I'm going to do it at my own pace. I'll do it when I'm ready, and I'll do it for good."

Now I was confused again, as I so often was when the subject of alcohol came up.

"Look, Jayway." I needed to marshal my thoughts. "If this were diabetes or dementia, we'd be getting help for you. This is similar but more dangerous. It will kill you, sooner or later."

"So, I'm going to stop. You know if I say I'll do something, I'll do it."

True, so far as it went. Yet he'd given up booze several times before and it hadn't lasted. He had to do something different this time.

"Here's the thing," I began. "I have three specific requests. We all want to help you quit permanently, and we know it's not easy." Jay started to demur, but I held up a hand. "I need you to do a four-to-five-day supervised detox."

I wasn't sure how he was taking this. His face seemed expressionless, or maybe it was a trick of the light.

"I want you to have regular counseling to help you through. Plus, if you find it hard to quit, there's a drug you can take." I couldn't think of the name right then.

Jay remained silent as he thought this over.

"Okay," he said eventually. "So long as I can choose when."

I had to concede something. If he felt I'd forced him to get sober, it would never stick. He had to be in control of his own recovery. All I could do was detach and try to trust that he would keep his word. The fact that he'd made a promise in front of the children gave me a small ray of hope.

❊ ❊ ❊

It was a couple of months before he put his favorite glass away in the back of the kitchen cabinet. We visited Mr. Sobieski, who referred us to Greenwich Hospital. Jay only stayed there for forty-eight hours since he hadn't had any withdrawal symptoms, he claimed. I believed him, because he'd never had them before, either. He was more inclined to be sleepy for the first couple of days, and then carried on with no visible side effects.

He never did go for the counseling part of the process.

I hoped we'd be able to negotiate the time we spent together, and where. It's not that I didn't want to be with him, I explained—I just didn't want to be with him when the man I'd fallen in love with, the real Jay Wilson, was lost in a vodka bottle.

He did manage to stay sober. At least for the next eighteen months.

Chapter 14
Ready to Divorce

Things between us had improved considerably while he was sober. I was more willing to be in New Hampshire, and we enjoyed being together. We visited local attractions, like the Simon Pearce glass-blowing factory and the historic home and garden of John Hay, Lincoln's private secretary. We did the local house tour at Christmas and admired the decorations, happy to be drinking hot cider instead of mulled wine.

Now that Jay wasn't drinking, he was more open to discussing our relationship and even understanding my point of view. I thought we were making progress.

So, the moment I lost hope for good will remain vividly imprinted on my memory. It was an early summer evening, around six o'clock, and the sun was beginning to set over the lake. I was slicing onions on a turquoise chopping board in the kitchen when Jay walked in and casually opened the cabinet by the fridge where we kept the liquor. He'd chosen this spot when we first built the house because it was next to the ice supply.

My heart missed a beat, but I carried on rhythmically moving the knife up and down.

"I thought I might have a glass of chardonnay."

All of a sudden, my mouth felt dry. Why? Why was he going to spoil everything now?

Because alcoholism is a cunning and baffling disease, as they say in AA.

"Darling, you know I can give up any time. I've been on the wagon for a year and a half, so it's obviously not an issue."

I remained silent.

"So, I thought one glass before dinner... nothing stronger... might be okay. I'm sure I can handle it."

I chose my words carefully, as though I were talking to someone armed and dangerous. "Well, it's your decision. But this could be the beginning of the slippery slope."

"Slippery slope? What do you mean?"

Of course, he knew. He must have known. Still, if this is how he was going to play it...

"You know they say one drink always leads to another."

"I'm not like that. I can quit any time."

I carried on cooking, too shocked and disappointed to cry. I could feel the ground falling away from me as the loving marriage I so longed for faded from sight.

❊ ❊ ❊

Months later, I was still trying. I'd invited some acquaintances over, and prepared a meal I hoped most people would like. Jay, in charge of the wine, had provided plenty of it. He felt he was still in control of his drinking if he wasn't drinking vodka. After a few glasses of cabernet, he told the story of how we'd first met, and about the affair we'd had while he was still married.

It wasn't something I liked to brag about, which he knew. I'd managed sometimes to make light of the fact that I was "the other woman," but in truth, I had some residual guilt about it, even though Jay's ex-wife was now happily remarried. I felt mortified to be cast as a femme fatale, though I tried to treat the subject lightly.

There wasn't any point in saying anything to him right then, but the next morning, I told him what had upset me: these weren't close friends, and he wouldn't stop when I attempted to deflect him, which made me feel stupid.

I forgave him, eventually, of course. Perhaps the story hadn't been so terrible, and in any case, embarrassment wasn't going to kill me, which was how I justified each decision to stay with him.

❀ ❀ ❀

Jay kept drinking and the problems kept piling up.

A day or two before Christmas, I was on my way back to Connecticut, my last planned trip before the holidays, which I'd be spending in New Hampshire, as I had for the last ten years. I needed a couple of days' break to fortify myself for the festivities. They always meant a great deal of work, since our family of six children with assorted spouses and partners, and six grandchildren would be invading the house over the holidays.

I liked to get together with them, but there would be a lot of meals, gifts, and activities to organize, and very little chance to regroup. Jay hadn't been pleased about my heading south, and I'd left with a feeling of relief tinged with anxiety.

In Claremont, near the Vermont border, a snowplow drove into my car.

The police officer, who arrived within minutes, checked my fender and gave it a yank to see if he could straighten it out. "I'll contact the tow guy for you." He held out the accident report.

In spite of the tension between us, I phoned Jay, who promised to come right away. I worried he'd already had a glass of something, but I had no one else to call. Thirty minutes later, his red pickup, which could handle any depth of snow, loomed up. When Jay bought it, he explained that he'd wanted one since he was a boy in Minnesota. He'd ordered a number plate saying, "MY TOY," just in case anyone was in doubt about it.

As he drove me back to New London, I stared out of the window and was grateful. I hadn't been hurt. Jay had come and had only been concerned about me, not the car. Tomorrow we'd find a rental. Though a thought nagged at me. Who would have fetched me if I were living alone?

The collision forced me to face the fact I was stretched too thin and needed to pay attention to my own welfare. Another accident might not end so well.

A week later, on Christmas Eve, Adam and his girlfriend drove up from Vermont and were late for dinner. My son apologized and explained to me privately that they'd had a row before they got to our house, which had caused the delay. Cell phone service was sketchy along the Vermont highways then, so he hadn't been able to call. Jay took them both into the den to vent his anger.

I could hear his raised voice from the hallway. I understood why he was annoyed, but this was ruining the evening. I didn't think he would have reacted the same way if he hadn't been drinking.

New Year's Eve proved to be the final straw. We'd invited a couple to eat with us and some of the children. They were interesting and fun, and the husband didn't drink, which made me think he might recognize Jay's problem. Things were going well until after dinner.

Sitting in front of the fire, after cocktails and a few glasses of wine, Jay began to tell the same story about our long-ago affair, implying that his irresistible charm had enticed me to bed. The fact that there was some truth in this was beside the point. It was something for Jay and me to share, not for the world to know. I watched the children melting away from the room as their discomfiture matched mine. My jaw tightened as I tried to smile.

Jay admitted much later that he knew he'd made a mistake. Yet he was unable to stop.

Waking early the next day, I grabbed my weekend bag and some of my clothes, leaving most behind—I had enough in Connecticut. Tossing in my laptop and a handful of books I'd been given for Christmas, I went to find my heavy-duty boots. Bitter northern winters would be behind me now, but practical footwear might come in useful.

I left without saying I wouldn't be coming back. I wasn't ready yet to deal with Jay's reaction, which I anticipated would be angry. First, I needed to discover what life without him would be like.

Pulling into the garage in Fairfield, I sat in the car, looking around at my bike, the toolbox, and my gardening tools, and let out a sigh of relief. I stretched as I stood there and walked through to the house.

Sunlight was filtering through the windows facing the short street I lived on. I could hear the two little boys across the way screaming with delight as they threw snowballs at each other. My neighbor Jim was shoveling about two inches of powder from his front path.

I thought for a moment about how beautiful New Hampshire could be when the sun sparkled on a new snowfall. Then I recalled the many times I'd felt trapped as my car spun its wheels in the icy driveway up there, or blizzards kept me housebound.

Unlike me, Jay relished being stuck in the house, plopped down in front of a roaring fire with a book, while the weather did its worst.

If there hadn't been a glass of vodka and tonic standing on the arm of his chair, I might have enjoyed that cozy domestic scene as well. I could have relaxed and been happy just to sit and read with the husband I loved nearby. But the man I'd married disappeared into the glass with the first vodka of the day, leaving behind someone who resembled him, yet who didn't notice whether I was there or not.

I had no fireplace in Connecticut, so after putting the kettle on, I went out to fetch my bags. By the time I'd taken them upstairs and reclaimed my side of the bed by bouncing up and down on it a couple of times, the water had boiled.

Downstairs, I placed my tea on the coffee table in the living room before falling into the welcoming comfort of my grandmother's sofa, brought over from England more than thirty years before. The bright red mug had been a gift from Barb and bore the very appropriate British slogan: *Stay Calm and Drink Tea.*

Gazing out at the garden, I took in the crystalline mantle covering most of the plants, but easily made out the shape of my temperamental apple tree, wondering if it might deign to provide some fruit this year. I was home.

It occurred to me I wouldn't be interrupted if I wanted to write, so I unpacked my journal, moved to my mother's old desk by the window, and began to take stock.

I had no one I needed to ring. Friends were used to my breezing in and out of town. When they asked me why Jay wasn't around much, I'd answer, not entirely joking, that occasionally we met in a gas station halfway between our two houses on Interstate 91. Now, of course, we wouldn't be doing even that.

❖ ❖ ❖

Connecticut friends became accustomed to the idea that I was more available to spend time with them. I found I could be happy alone too—striding along the sidewalks of New York to theatres, museums, and galleries, or seeing friends. Single neighbors and I were able to go to the movies at a couple of hours' notice. At last, with nobody else to take into account, I was allowing myself to be the person I always felt like inside.

Jay phoned once or twice, under the pretext of asking how the washing machine worked, or where he could find a particular jacket. We were civil, but he called me Gabi, so I could tell he was angry.

Three weeks after I'd left Sunset Shores, the day before my birthday, I drove back to New Hampshire. I'd made arrangements to meet with a lawyer in Concord and then to collect my Prius, now as good as new after the accident, and pick up a few things from the lake house. Jay wouldn't be there—he was away on business.

Aware I'd need an attorney, I'd done some research. Ann Schiffman billed herself as a mediated divorce lawyer, which sounded appropriate to me. Or at least not as bad as an adversarial one. The more Ann and I talked, the more I realized how destructive a divorce might be, not only for us but for the family.

We would likely have to sell Sunset Shores, which would mean Jay's home, the place where the family gathered, would be gone. The children might feel they needed to be loyal to one or the other of us. The grandchildren would miss seeing us together.

I decided that if we could arrange to live apart amicably, and I continued to receive an allowance, we might make this much easier on ourselves. Relief washed over me as I made the decision. I didn't hate my husband—I simply couldn't live with him anymore.

❋ ❋ ❋

Back in Connecticut, flashes of guilt clouded my days because I was enjoying my new freedom so much. I could tell, by the chill in his voice when he called me once or twice a week, that Jay wasn't coming to terms with any of this. It had probably been too much to expect that he would. Every few weeks, he would show up on his way to his dentist in

Greenwich, or to business meetings in New York or Washington.

Seeing him come through the front door one early spring day, his face set in a tight-lipped mask, I steeled myself to be as British as I could, polite and friendly but not too affectionate.

Jay poured himself a vodka and tonic from the supplies he'd brought with him and came to perch on one of the small armchairs in the living room. He didn't look comfortable.

I guess we both knew this wouldn't be an easy conversation. He launched right in.

"You know I love you, don't you?" His eyes were locked on mine. "I've never stopped loving you."

I wasn't convinced. He loved me the best way he could, but I was only second in his affections. The bottle would always win out.

"I know," I said. "I love you too."

"So why are you doing this?"

I had nothing new to say. We were on old ground, now.

"You know why." I wasn't going to talk about drinking if I could help it. "I can't live in New Hampshire permanently." I shivered at the thought. "You're not prepared for us to split the time we spend in each place. I've been coming up there three or four days a week, and the eight-hour round trip is time when I could be writing, or seeing my friends."

I was taking writing classes and had started a monthly group for writers in the local Barnes & Noble bookstore. I wrote a blog where I posted ideas and tips on writing and publishing. Friends with subscriptions to theatres in Hartford, New Haven, and Westport invited me to go with them. This was only part of the reason I needed a compromise.

It wasn't only about being in New Hampshire – it was about living with an alcoholic in New Hampshire. For me, marriage meant sharing a life, putting each other first, and making a real effort to make the relationship work. I'd been trying to do that for years but often felt I was swimming against the tide.

I leaned toward him, willing him to understand me this time. "I wish we could spend time together in *both* places but that won't happen, will it?" All of a sudden, I ran out of steam.

I pushed a small bowl of nuts across the coffee table, but he shook his head.

"I guess, Gabi, what you're saying is you won't move there full-time to be with me." It wasn't a question.

"Right, Jay. But that's nothing new."

Calling each other by our given names, rather than by a nickname, showed we were angry.

"So, how can we make this work?"

There was no getting around the problem. I would have to make it clear, once and for all. "I don't think we can, do you? Neither of us is ready to give in, now."

Jay wouldn't quit, though. "What if we find ways to be together more, talk over our issues and what we want from each other?"

"We've tried that, and it always ends in a stalemate."

"I think you expect too much from me. I mean, I accept your imperfections, yet you won't reciprocate." He frowned as he took an absent-minded handful of nuts from the dish.

I saw no point in answering this. He was talking about his drinking. That's what he wanted me to accept, but it was causing too large a wedge between us. It hurt that, when it came right down to it, he would choose alcohol over me, but he saw my stance as obsessing over something trivial. He refused to understand how I felt about this one huge issue.

"I love you, Jay, but I can't live with you. It's just too exhausting."

He bit down hard on the cashews, grinding his teeth unnecessarily.

"Have you been to see a divorce lawyer?"

I admitted I had.

"I don't think that's the answer," I said. "All the legal stuff would be very disruptive for both of us, and for the family. You might have to sell Sunset Shores, which I know you love."

I wondered if he'd considered this, but decided it was unlikely he'd even begun to imagine how a divorce might impact his way of life.

I offered an olive twig.

"Listen, I'm prepared to participate in family events and holidays, but I want to live on my own the rest of the time."

Abruptly, he changed the subject.

"What do we do about Russia, then?"

I'd forgotten about the two-week river cruise we had booked months ago. Maybe I could manage to be with him for two weeks? I'd always wanted to go there, and we both enjoyed traveling. Only when we traveled together did we achieve some sort of harmony. Jay reveled in sampling luxurious accommodations and food, and I delighted in trying to speak an unfamiliar language and learning about a new culture. Our differences receded once we were on neutral turf.

"Let me think about it." Pros and cons flashed through my mind. "Perhaps we could still do that."

He had a final question for me as he left to go back to the lake house.

"Gabi, tell me one thing. Is there someone else?"

I felt sorry for him at that point. He really couldn't understand why anyone would choose to forgo a life of comfort with him in New Hampshire, to hang out alone in a tiny house in a small Connecticut town. Put that way, I suppose it must have seemed irrational.

Still, the very fact that he had so often ignored my pleas

for him to get and stay sober, reflected his single-mindedness. We became entrenched in our own positions, and now we wouldn't compromise. He wanted me in New London. I needed to be in Fairfield—and neither of us was prepared to give up our dream.

I shook my head.

"There's no one else. Just me."

As he slammed the front door on his way out, I collapsed back onto the sofa I'd known since my childhood and let tears of sorrow and relief roll down my cheeks.

✽ ✽ ✽

We declared an uneasy truce and went to Russia in June. It wasn't a success. We returned home more alienated than ever. Jay, by this time frustrated by his inability to bring me to heel, lost his temper with anything beyond his control. When the tour guides wanted us to return to the ship before he was ready, when our flight from St. Petersburg was delayed and we missed our connection in London, he took it out on the airport staff—and me.

Our claustrophobic cabin made being together even more difficult. His recurring stomach aches didn't help. I put it down to a different diet and too many vodka tastings.

Afterward, Jay hunkered down in New Hampshire, and I returned to Connecticut. But when plans were made for July Fourth weekend, I agreed to show up.

✽ ✽ ✽

The idea was to celebrate Jay's birthday as well as July 4th, since the family would be together. Jay was difficult to buy presents for, so our two sons, Fred and Bertie, had come up with an original idea. I was always urging them to think in terms of experiences, rather than gifts, so instead of buying him yet another golf gadget or something for his barbecue, they bought him a pig.

Not a live one, one they would cook. My heart sank as I heard this. I'm a vegetarian, so a dead pig in my kitchen was my concept of hell. They told Jay about it in advance, since a pig roast is not something to spring on a person. He was delighted, telling everyone he'd be the medieval lord whose minions would appear with a roast suckling pig, apple in its mouth, on a platter.

A huge amount of planning went into producing this gift. Fred is a perfectionist and was in charge of procuring the animal. He trawled the Internet, made phone calls, and all in all, behaved as though he were arranging a blind date on match.com.

He came into the kitchen one day and smugly announced he'd found the object of his desire.

"It's small," he explained. "Plus, it's been running around on a mountain in Vermont until just recently."

This was to persuade me the pig had had a good life before becoming pork.

"It's a Mainline Cross, so Tamworth with a pinch of Gloucester Old Spot and Hampshire," he went on. Apparently, in addition to match.com, he'd checked on Ancestry.com. "About thirty pounds. I have to go and collect it next Thursday. It's only a hundred and twenty miles away, so it shouldn't be a problem. I'll have to get a big enough cooler, of course," he mused. "And lots of ice." I handed him a sheet of paper and a pen. This might turn out to be a long list.

I was trying not to think about the fact that this animal was about the weight of an overweight border collie.

"So, what's its name?" I asked.

Fred's eyebrows shot up.

"Well, looks like you know everything else about it," I teased.

Fred gave me up as an audience and strode off to find

a container suitable for his project. In due course, he returned from a day trip to Vermont with a huge blue and white cooler in the back of his small Prius. Fred is six feet four and very strong, and even he couldn't manage this on his own, so he enlisted Jay to help him carry it into the mudroom.

In the meantime, his brother Bertie was arranging for all the paraphernalia required for a pig roast. When he arrived on the Saturday morning of July 5, his car, too, was laden with stuff.

Bertie dragged out the contents with the panache of a conjurer pulling rabbits out of a hat. He hauled into the house an enormous portable barbecue pit, several sacks of charcoal, some smaller bags of mesquite chips, plastic utensils and glasses, paper plates and napkins, appropriately decorated with a border of bright red pigs. His girlfriend Julia, here for the day to support him, carried in the beer, the potato salad, and the coleslaw.

I tried to be helpful. "Shall I put out some apple sauce?"

Bertie snorted. "This isn't an English Sunday lunch," he said patiently.

I was forced to agree.

I hid in the bedroom when it was time to heave the cooler outside and slide the pig onto the spit. I'd made the boys position it somewhere on the terrace where it would be beyond my line of sight. Though like toddlers who've made some mud pies or a sandcastle, they'd come up to me at intervals to ask if I'd like to come and check it out.

"I'm sure it's lovely." I hoped I sounded convincing.

Jay walked over from time to time to tell them how thrilled he was and how well it was coming along, but I noticed he was pale beneath his tan.

When lunch was ready, sometime in mid-afternoon, the boys proudly carved some pork and distributed it to our guests. There were only thirteen people there to eat the damn thing.

I ate the salad I'd prepared and tried not to look at the pig, still slowly turning, because it wasn't cooked through.

* * *

Jay had always enjoyed his food. His six-foot-two frame had supported some 200-230 pounds over the decades we'd been married. He'd sometimes decide to lose weight and did this by skipping lunch, apparently with no ill effects. I could only watch with envy. If I missed my midday meal, I became irritable.

He'd been eating fairly well over the summer, but since the Russian trip, he'd been suffering from what he thought was frequent and particularly violent indigestion. I wasn't so sure. Indigestion and heartburn had been a standard feature of his life for years, and Jay powered through it with antacids. Yet it seemed increasingly painful as the days passed.

That day, Jay was fulsome in his praise for the pig, the boys, the day, the weather, and the company. But before long, he slipped away to find some antacid. It didn't work, really, but the children never knew.

We'd booked flights to Montana to meet old friends in August. I hesitated to travel with him again so soon, but I wanted to spend some time with the Sargents, because Helen was dying of breast cancer, after being in remission for many years.

So, when Jay, who normally had a high pain threshold, phoned me in Connecticut to say he needed to cancel because his stomach felt so bad, I realized it was significant. This was the guy who once traveled to New Zealand with a broken leg, so keen was he not to miss the trip.

"They've done a couple of tests and haven't found anything." That sounded positive, at least. Then he added, "So they want to do a colonoscopy next week. Can you take me?"

I sighed inwardly, but since we'd canceled Montana, my calendar was empty, so I agreed to drive up to New Hampshire.

I didn't know then that I would have to spend every day of the next seven months in the house I'd finally walked away from.

And I certainly never expected to fall in love with Jay again.

PART THREE
RETURN TO LOVE

Death—or the prospect of death—has a way of
clearing away everything that is not real.
— *Elizabeth Gilbert*

Chapter 15
Diagnosis

Sunday, August 24, 2014

I drove up to New Hampshire, planning to stay for the weekend, make the most of the perfect late summer weather, and drive Jay to his appointment and back. He didn't look well.

Over the next twenty-four hours, I registered how much he'd deteriorated since our most recent encounter. I'd never seen him so lacking in energy. He wasn't a malingerer, so I figured this must be serious. Just not too terrible, I prayed to a God I didn't believe in.

His face, normally a healthy color, would turn white almost every hour now, as he pressed his lips together, trying to deny the pain. He hadn't managed to force down much food since I'd been there.

As the day went on, I became more and more anxious. I tried to pretend I hadn't noticed anything wrong, so as not to worry him.

I walked into the bathroom, where his colonoscopy prep materials were lined up on the counter. Then I made a decision.

"I'm not letting you do this at home." I would not give

way on this. "You're already weak, and this will only make it worse. If you get dehydrated and collapse, I won't be able to help you up again."

Even though he was thinner than before, Jay was no lightweight. I expected an argument, but he said nothing.

"So, if they want to do a colonoscopy," I went on. "They can supervise you at the hospital."

I drove him to the emergency room.

He told them about what they insisted on calling his "abdominal discomfort." I explained my fears around the colonoscopy, the previous tests, and his lack of energy. They gave him a morphine-based drug to make him more comfortable and finally agreed to admit him.

❀ ❀ ❀

Tuesday, August 26

The colonoscopy showed nothing, so they decided to do one more CT scan, just in case. This time they would use a contrast dye, which they hadn't previously, because of Jay's allergy to iodine. To prevent a reaction, they gave him a course of prednisone, which meant another 24-hour delay.

We'd have to wait until Thursday for the results.

❀ ❀ ❀

Thursday, August 28

At ten past eight in the morning, I ran my hand under the antiseptic gel dispenser in the hospital hallway and walked as fast as I could toward the ward. I'd overslept—lying in bed dreaming about buying art and living in a flat high above the river in London, my hometown. None of it made much sense.

I found Jay in the sunny hospital room where I'd left him, sitting up in a bed strewn with yesterday's newspapers, which he seemed to have abandoned. A single page, folded several times, lay on his bedside table, near a half-completed Sudoku puzzle. I went to the end of the bed and bent to put down my bag, before giving him a quick kiss. Right now, Jay didn't look as though he was in any pain. He smiled at me.

Gail, a friendly nurse, was standing with her back to the door, tapping at the computer on its stand. She turned around as she heard me come in.

"Just entering the meds." She gave me a smile.

"When's the doctor expected?" I asked.

"Oh," she said, making for the door, "he's already been. About half an hour ago."

"What?"

I wanted to scream with frustration. I'd deliberately planned to arrive at the hospital so as not to miss the doctor, who was to begin his rounds at eight. As I was leaving the evening before, I'd told the nurse on duty I absolutely had to be there when they gave Jay the results of his CT scan the next day.

My husband had always been the type of patient who never bothered with medical jargon, and as a result, never questioned doctors about anything. I, on the other hand, found the antidote to anxiety was information. I was the skeptical one, the one who asked why, and what and how. That was my role. I took a deep breath. I needed to keep calm, on the outside at least.

"So, what did he say?" I asked.

"Your husband will tell you."

The morning sun was streaming in through the window, and beyond, a gentle breeze was moving the treetops, making me glad we were in this rural hospital, and not in some urban setting where the view would likely consist of a brick wall.

"They found something." Jay's tone was neutral.

The sun continued to shine, but I felt a cold shiver run down my back. I tried a laugh.

"You're kidding, right?"

He smiled at me, but I could tell there was nothing funny about this.

"He thinks it's pancreatic cancer. But he doesn't think it's spread," he said.

My voice sounded distant. "Not spread. That's good, right?"

Of *course* this wasn't good. It was terrible.

My mind went spiraling down in a jumble of thoughts. Fuck. Pancreatic cancer. So, no hope of a cure. No one to help Jay through it but me. This was so unfair. I saw my chances of returning to my new life in Connecticut receding fast. Might we be able to hire people to give him a hand? Fuck again.

But perhaps he'd recover. In any case, he wouldn't be an invalid, would he? He'd cope. I shook my head to clear it and moved up the bed to take his hand—warm and dry, as always. It was a hand I had always loved to hold, though we hadn't held hands in a long time.

"Are they sure? How can they be sure?" I asked.

"That little doctor, you know the one?"

I nodded.

"He says they have to do a biopsy to be certain, but he thinks that's what it is."

I grasped at a tiny straw. So, it wasn't definite then. "That little doctor" had been wrong before. He'd done a CT scan a couple of weeks ago and seen nothing. So, whatever they'd found, it must be minuscule.

"They want to do it as soon as possible."

❖ ❖ ❖

Friday, August 29

I sat in Jay's cubicle at Dartmouth-Hitchcock Medical Center, waiting for him to come back from the endoscopic ultrasound, which had necessitated a general anesthetic. He'd been at the endoscopy unit a month before, when they carried out a similar procedure that hadn't revealed anything. Now they were actively searching for trouble.

I waited, both for him to come round properly, and for the doctor, who'd promised to let us know what he found. I had a cup of coffee and a book with me, but I kept reading and re-reading the same page without taking anything in. The harder I tried not to think about what Jay was going through, the more agitating thoughts intruded. What would we do when the test came back positive? What if it were untreatable? God, how I hated hospitals.

They wheeled him back into the room, groggy but determined to wake up. About forty minutes later, he was sitting up and sipping at some juice when the surgeon slid open the glass door of the cubicle and entered with a file under his arm.

He was young, tall, and slim, and I couldn't read his face. I searched for signs of discomfort, or maybe a cheerful smile, which would give me some sort of clue, but I could discern nothing in his warm but non-committal expression.

Jay turned to face him and asked for the news. I took hold of his hand. Clearing his throat, the doctor told us that, based on the pathologist's first impressions of the biopsy, he was 99.9 percent sure it was malignant.

We were silent for a moment. I squeezed Jay's hand gently. I didn't know what else to do. Then Jay nodded slowly. I think part of him had known for a while that he wouldn't be able to tough it out this time.

"What are our options?" he asked, beginning the long journey by talking as if we both had the disease. He was right, of course; this would be our odyssey, not just his. I wouldn't let Jay face this without me by his side.

The doctor explained that his secretary was setting up meetings as we sat there, first with the oncologist, who would work out a plan of treatment, and then with the team who'd be carrying it out. The chemo, or whatever it would be, would start in a matter of days.

"What about a second opinion?" Though he accepted their diagnosis, I think Jay wondered if there might be more than one way to treat it. Possibly some famous clinic would be able to do a better job.

But when I thought of flying to hospitals in faraway states, and the toll that would take on both of us, I prayed he would decide to stay here.

"You're perfectly welcome to do that, of course," said the young doctor. "We can give you contacts at all the chief places: Memorial Sloan Kettering, the Mayo, and the Cleveland." Jay nodded, doubtless liking the sound of the big guns being deployed on his behalf. He believed in the maxim that one got what one paid for.

"I still think you should meet our team. Some of our doctors are from MSK, and one of them trained under the most famous and respected pancreatic cancer surgeon in the country."

Jay was relieved, I think, to have a diagnosis at last. In a way, I was, too. Now we had identified the problem, we could begin to fix it. Like many men, his favored way of dealing with a disaster was to find a practical solution. He didn't have much time to waste on feelings in these kinds of circumstances. I guess that was my automatic response, too. Only action would help me feel better.

To keep us busy and feeling as though something was happening, they promised to have us meet the medical team as soon as possible. The first appointment, the admissions meeting, was scheduled for Tuesday—the day after Labor Day. They were to explain all the options for treating the disease, and the ways in which they might help with the anticipated collateral shock to friends and family.

The second date was for the week after, when the treatment would begin.

I found one saving grace in this moment. As cleanly as the cut of a surgeon's knife, I stopped thinking about living in Connecticut and simply accepted that Jay needed me now. And I needed to be with him, too. He was the love of my life, and I wasn't about to let him take this journey alone.

***

I try to avoid regrets in my life. When major decisions are called for, I make up my mind according to whether I'll regret either doing, or failing to do, something. Luckily, my choices aren't cast in stone. I thought I wanted to be as far away from my husband and New Hampshire as possible. Now I knew I'd regret it if I didn't stay.

And just like that, I stepped onto the path that would change both our lives.

Chapter 16
Labor Day Weekend

We had to tell the children. Theoretically, we might be termed a blended family, but, in practice, there's nothing truly blended about us. No velvety, creamy liquid like a power smoothie. Ours is more like a chunky gazpacho, where the predominant flavor depends on who's making soup on any given day.

Now, more than thirty years after our wedding, Amanda lived an hour and a half away, in a suburb of Boston, with her wife Barb and their two children, Ellie and Max.

Heather, married to Ned, lived in Connecticut with him and their two girls. She had grown up the more conventional of the two sisters, a woman bound by tradition, continuity, and family beyond anything else. She was easy to talk to and talented at drawing people out, so she was familiar with my concerns over her dad, and I wondered how this would affect her.

Helenka was supposed to be coming up with her two daughters for the Labor Day weekend. Improbably, she was now a teacher, an excellent one, so this would be her last chance of a few days off before school started again.

But it had been less than twenty-four hours since the

diagnosis, and neither of us felt like having grandchildren around. It was hard enough to get to grips with the news, without having to organize meals and entertain little ones. If they came, I'd have to pretend nothing was wrong, because Jay didn't want me to tell anyone he had cancer yet—he wanted to let people know himself.

"What shall we do about Amanda and Heather?" I asked Jay. "They want to hear about the results, and they'll probably want to come up and see you. They'll have to make arrangements about the kids."

We called the girls, and they came up the following day. Generally, I found having people to stay in New Hampshire a chore, but this time I was glad they were there. Planning meals and making beds gave me something to do, and it was reassuring for their dad to know they cared and would show up when he needed them.

❊ ❊ ❊

Saturday, August 30

The weather was perfect, the lake serene in the early evening as we sat on the stone terrace that looked across the water to the Loon Lighthouse. Jay had taken some of the medication he'd been prescribed, so he wasn't in pain, and was sipping on a vodka, cranberry juice, and tonic, his current drink of choice.

The girls, as we had continued to call them, even though they were in their forties, had brought elegant little snacks, and they and I nibbled at them while they drank a glass of wine each and listened.

"They don't think it's spread." Absent-mindedly, Jay stirred his cocktail with his forefinger to make sure it was mixed properly. As it turned out, I think that may have been the last alcoholic drink he ever had, though neither of us knew it then.

Jay was focusing on what we hoped was the good news, partly for the girls, and also to reinforce his own positive take on the situation. In reality, the doctors weren't sure whether or not the cancer had metastasized, and had scheduled another CT scan the day after Labor Day to find out. I followed up on Jay's comment.

"The tumor is in an awkward spot, so they need to shrink it before they can operate."

The spot wasn't just awkward. I could tell. It would be impossible to operate on. I'd studied the photos of the cancer, which Jay had only glanced at, and I could see the tumor was clinging to two arteries. So, an operation would be much too dangerous.

I looked at the girls. Heather, whose every emotion was visible on her face, was biting her lip, trying to hold herself together. Amanda, older by three years, was more accustomed to keeping her feelings in check—toughing it out—like her father. But she couldn't hide her anxious frown and the trepidation in her eyes.

"Dartmouth has a great reputation," Jay went on.

"We're going to see the team on Tuesday," I added. "They can start treatment more or less immediately."

"How bad *is* it?" asked Amanda, wanting some sense of the magnitude of the problem.

"It's only the size of a nickel." He held up his finger and thumb to illustrate.

The tumor wasn't the size of a nickel. It was about four centimeters across—bigger than a silver dollar. There was no point in saying so, though.

"What will they do?" Heather wanted to know.

"As Gabi said, they'll likely do some radiation treatment to shrink it before they can operate."

He was going with the best-case scenario, and I couldn't blame him. Not for the first time, I wondered whether he'd actually taken in the truth.

"Dinner will be ready in a minute." I left them to it.

✻ ✻ ✻

Sunday, August 31

I groaned as I opened my eyes the next morning. Jay was still asleep, but I remembered the girls were staying and dragged myself out of bed to find them something for breakfast.

We'd had a fractured night, after Jay woke me at three-fifteen with a severe muscle spasm in his leg. I massaged it, made him drink some liquids, and gave him an Advil and a couple of homeopathic remedies. Nothing helped, so I phoned the hospital. The nurse on duty agreed that it sounded like cramp, and told me I could increase his pain meds. After a while, he went back to sleep, and once I heard his steady breathing, I did, too.

Amanda, Heather, and I were hanging out in the kitchen, waiting for their dad to wake up, and I was reporting on our broken night. The girls made sympathetic noises.

"Hey," said Heather. "I'm thinking, since it's Labor Day weekend and I don't have to be back home until tomorrow night, I could stay over and help."

She handed me a mug of tea, brewed strong, the way I like it. I took it gratefully and sat down at the dining room table. The lake beyond was a peaceful blue, as though nothing extraordinary were happening.

"I think I may be able to stay, too." Amanda's face was paler than usual. "I'll call Barb and check."

The offer of help gave me some options. It occurred to me that this might provide my only chance to get down to Fairfield for a while. I'd arrived in New Hampshire with only enough clothes for a few days, and had left all my papers and books behind. I asked the girls if they'd mind keeping their father company while I drove down, stayed overnight, and came back the next day. I told them Jay hadn't had a recurrence of the cramp and appeared to be sleeping peacefully now.

It was a lovely drive, a late summer's day around eighty degrees. I had an audiobook to listen to, so although I had a lot on my mind, I felt for a time that I was being given a short break from it.

Three hours later, the sun was dropping in the sky, and I was about forty minutes from the Connecticut home when Amanda called. Jay's leg had turned blue and they had taken him to the New London emergency room. The ER personnel had diagnosed an arterial embolism, a blood clot. He would require an operation, most likely tomorrow.

My mind went into shock, and I found myself thinking and acting on auto-pilot. I decided that since I was so close to home, and there was nothing I could do right now, I'd continue to Fairfield, pick up my things, and go back the same day.

I walked into the house, my brain buzzing with worry about Jay's leg, wondering who'd look after the place if I wasn't there, and making a mental list of things I would need to take back with me.

I headed up to the attic bedroom, and into the stifling heat under the eaves. The air conditioning hadn't been on since I'd left. There wasn't much point in turning it on now.

I threw some clothes and shoes into a couple of bags. My anti-depressants and blood pressure medication went in, too. This was no time to stop taking them. In my office, I scooped up the writing I was working on and stuffed it into a weekend bag with a few books from my to-be-read pile.

Might I need my passport? We were supposed to be going to Montreal later in the month. I grabbed it just in case. I rescued what I could from the fridge, packed a box of English tea bags, and tossed it all into the back of the car before pulling out of the driveway.

I'd finished my audiobook and was listening to my playlist of sad songs, always guaranteed to make me weep if I needed to—I must have cried for over an hour. It began to rain as I crossed the border into Vermont—spitting at first, then showers, and rain, and spitting again. It was still daylight though the skies were grim and gray. I was on cruise control doing about seventy-five when a sudden downpour took me by surprise, and I felt my little car begin to hydroplane.

The highway was shifting beneath me as I braked—I was sliding onto the grass verge. I wrenched the wheel into the skid and managed to get back on the road before over-correcting and ending up in the weeds again, tall sumacs looming up, wet and green, above me. I tried to breathe as I turned the wheel one more time and let the car find its footing back onto the tarmac.

As I shuddered to a stop, there was a thudding sound from the passenger side, and I realized that I had a flat tire, although everything else seemed to be working. I was three miles from the nearest exit, so I crawled along the shoulder until I reached it and pulled into a Sunoco station.

I sat and breathed for a minute, taking stock as I stared out of the windscreen at the raindrops, still racing down. I took out my phone to call Fred. He wasn't at home, so I tried his cell, and he promised to be there in thirty minutes. I cursed myself for messing up just half an hour away from my goal, then thanked God there was someone who could come to my rescue.

It was still raining as I got out to survey the damage. Both passenger-side tires were shredded; the wheel hubs were filled with earth and grass, as was the front grille. It looked as though the car had been competing in an off-road rally, and the mud line came halfway up the door.

Blades of grass festooned the whole car as if some crazy

person had made a demented attempt to decorate for a harvest festival. The passenger-side bumper was torn off, and I suspected the axles were damaged too.

Oh, well, it might be worse, I thought. It's only a car. At least no one had been hurt. But I was aware I'd had a lucky escape.

There was nothing I could do about getting it repaired on the Sunday of a Labor Day weekend, but I decided to leave a message for Mr. Stone, who'd fixed my car in January. Meanwhile, I collected my things, stuffing them into the empty shopping bags I always kept in the trunk, and walked into the gas station to ask if I could park there until Tuesday. When she heard my story, the cashier agreed the car could stay.

"Mr. Stone says he'll come and get it on Tuesday," I told her.

"Jim Stone? I know him. No problem."

Sometimes living in a small community where everyone knew everyone else was a good thing.

Fred arrived, explaining he'd been in the Dartmouth ER with Jay, Amanda, and Heather when I phoned. He drove me there with rain still pelting down, making me cringe at the speed we were going. I shut my eyes and clung to the door handle, saying nothing.

Jay looked tired, of course, but pleased to see me. I explained that I'd had a flat, which was why Fred had come to get me. There wasn't any point in worrying him unnecessarily right now.

Once they had Jay settled, and sleepy from the pain medications, the girls left for their respective homes. Fred gave me a ride back to Sunset Shores, and I collapsed into bed, falling instantly asleep. The operation was set for tomorrow, and I'd need to be on top of things.

❧ ❧ ❧

Monday, September 1 – Labor Day

I woke early, jittery with worry. I was glad the girls had left. They had their families to get back to, and I was finding it increasingly hard to be reassuring and optimistic in the face of their contagious anxiety.

Dragging on a clean pair of jeans and a T-shirt, I slapped some gloss across my lips, grabbed a cup of tea and a peach, and ran out of the house. I had half an hour to reach the hospital by seven, to talk to the surgeon before the operation. I had questions—I needed the reassurance that this was strictly routine, that Jay wasn't likely to die from it, and that he'd be up and about within a day or two.

In the bowels of the hospital, along endless corridors with too much fluorescent lighting, I followed the gurney as they took him to the operating theater. He seemed vulnerable in the blue paper shower cap he was wearing, but he smiled gamely as I pretended this was just a routine procedure.

When the vascular surgeon walked up, I was hard-pressed to accept that this young man would know what to do with my husband, and I guess my anxiety showed as I plied him with questions, stalling for time before they wheeled Jay away, and there'd be nothing more I could do. The surgeon took his time with me, patiently putting me at ease.

"So, when can he come home?" I needed to focus on the positive aspects of this operation.

"We send patients home as soon as they can walk unaided from the bed to the bathroom," he said. "Mostly in a day, or at most, two."

That sounded good to me. What I didn't understand was that the operation would require three incisions. So, walking to the bathroom, which should be so simple, wasn't necessarily going to be easy.

The anesthesiologist arrived to take Jay into the

operating theater.

"I'll see you after, darling." I smiled encouragingly. He just nodded, and I could see the strain in his eyes. He gave me a crooked smile and a small wave as he was wheeled away. I followed him with my eyes, until the heavy OR doors swung closed. I couldn't do anything now, except wait. I hoped he was in good hands.

The waiting room, painted a disheartening gray, did at least have a couple of recliners for anxious relatives like me. I could smell coffee somewhere and asked the volunteer receptionist where I could get some.

"There's a machine over here." She pointed, emerging from behind her desk. She was tiny and wrinkled, but had a reassuring smile. I supposed she'd seen all kinds of waiting relatives in this room—from stoics like me to people who fell apart.

I carried the small paper cup back to my seat, concentrating so as not to spill it, but abandoned it after one mouthful. I longed for a cup of strong tea—the kind my mother always swore by as the antidote to shock and disaster.

One of the people in the recliners had left while I was making coffee, so I nabbed it and tried to relax, but the dramatic events of the last few days overwhelmed me, and I started to cry. So much for stoicism.

The volunteer receptionist came over with a small box of hospital tissues.

"You can keep these." She pressed them into my hand.

❉ ❉ ❉

A computer tracked which patient was where in the surgical process. Activities were color-coded to show whether they were in surgery, in recovery, or available for relatives to visit. The bright colors were pretty, but waiting for them to change was nerve-wracking. I could see a monitor from where I sat, and when Jay's name came up as being out of the OR, I walked up to the receptionist to ask how long it might be before I could see him and/or the surgeon.

"Shouldn't be long," she said. "I'll let you know the minute he comes up on the screen."

It was long—well over an hour—before the surgeon finally appeared, taking his little paper hat off as he came through the doors marked "No Entry."

"Everything's gone well." I searched his face to try and detect any sign of ambivalence. "We took care of the embolism, and he should be ready to see you in about an hour."

I knew better than to complain that this was too long to wait, so I thanked him and returned to the recliner, where, anxiety allayed for a while, I dozed off.

❋ ❋ ❋

Tuesday, September 2

A day later, as promised, Jay was on his feet and able to walk far enough, using a walker, to let him come home. It was also the date of our first appointment with the medical team. Jay was in the surgical ward, still recovering from the operation, but neither of us wanted this to delay his treatment.

I walked out of the room to find a doctor so I could straighten things out. I sought out one of the interns on the floor and poured the story into her ear. "I'm sure we could get to the cancer center somehow, couldn't we?" I said.

She put a hand on my sleeve. "I understand your concern. I'll find out whether they can manage to see you today since you've missed the appointment time."

"I can push him there in a wheelchair," I offered.

"Let me see what I can arrange."

I watched her walk away. An hour later, she returned to say it wouldn't be possible.

My eyes filled with tears of frustration again, and I didn't try to stop them. If I was going to have a meltdown, I might as well do it to get what I needed for Jay. I took a deep breath.

"We are not going to leave this hospital until we've seen a doctor from the oncology department," I insisted, allowing the tears to trickle down my cheeks. "I can't do this to him. He's been through so much already."

The doctor gave my arm a squeeze.

"Try not to get upset, Mrs. Wilson. Perhaps I can get someone from the palliative care team to see you."

"But isn't palliative care for people who are terminal?" I felt a cold hand grip my stomach. Surely, it was much too early for that?

"No, no." She shook her head with conviction. Her blond ponytail swung behind her. "It's for anyone who's chronically ill. I'll have the head of the team, Donna Santoro, come and see you if she can. She'll explain it all."

I had no idea what part palliative care might have to play in cancer treatment, but it was better than nothing, so I dried my eyes and went back to Jay's room to report some success.

Donna came in an hour or so later with a smile and a packet of information under one arm. Like all the other medical staff we'd met so far, she introduced herself with a handshake, after she'd run her hand under the sanitizer. I stood up to let her have my chair and sat on the side of the bed.

She explained that palliative care was concerned with the comfort of the patient and their family. It could begin as soon as someone was diagnosed. The palliative care doctors would monitor Jay's pain levels, making sure he was pain-free.

They could also provide spiritual guidance—Jay's expression told Donna all she needed to know about his interest in spiritual care—and complementary treatments like massage and, surprisingly, music therapy. They stayed in touch with the oncologists throughout to make sure medications didn't interact with each other.

"I've spoken to the cancer center." Her voice held a note of hope. "They'll be able to see you next Tuesday. I expect you'll be feeling a lot better by then."

❉ ❉ ❉

As part of the decision to let Jay go home, the doctor wanted to know if I'd be all right with changing the dressings on his legs, as necessary.

"I think I can manage that." I hoped I was right. "But I'd feel better if someone could come and check on him from time to time."

"We can have the local visiting nurses come," said the doctor, much to my relief. Having already failed to realize Jay had an embolism, I was nervous about missing some other important symptom.

"We'll set them up for three times a week, to begin with."

That turned out to be a blessing.

Chapter 17
On a Scale of One to Ten

Jay let out a breath between clenched teeth as he sat down, somewhat awkwardly, in the passenger seat of the car. "Thank God that's over. I've had enough of hospital beds and food to last me a while."

"Would you like a cup of proper coffee?" By which I meant the half regular, half decaf, brewed hazelnut beverage only available from Jake's convenience store at our local gas station. This was his favorite kind.

He brightened considerably. "Thanks, that'd be great."

We left the coffee in the cup holder while I helped Jay maneuver into the house. I backed his car into the garage so the passenger door was closer to the kitchen, hoping to God I wouldn't scratch anything. My own Prius was much smaller, but you had to reverse my husband's vehicle just so, to get it in.

It must have been painful, but Jay managed to limp inside without a problem. I was glad I'd insisted on having all the most-used rooms, including our bedroom, on the first floor of the house. When it was being built, I suggested to Jay we would save on heating and cooling costs upstairs when we were there on our own.

What I didn't say aloud was that there might come a time when we wouldn't be able to manage the stairs. Now, that day was here.

* * *

Wednesday, September 3

Beth, the nurse assigned as our case manager by the local Visiting Nurses Association, showed up early on Wednesday morning. Her freckled face wore a permanently anxious expression and was surrounded by reddish-blond wavy hair caught back in a colored elastic band, evidently designed to keep it in order. She wore jeans and a flowered shirt, and removed her hiking boots at the front door.

Across the lake, the newly risen sun was illuminating Mount Ascutney, almost thirty miles away in Vermont. As I led her through the sitting room, she exclaimed at the view, something all visitors did on first seeing it. Even I, who knew it so well, never tired of its beauty, different each day—each hour.

In the bedroom, she introduced herself to Jay, who was sitting back in bed, reading yesterday's papers, since I hadn't had a chance to get today's yet.

She unzipped her heavy shoulder bag and pulled out a laptop computer while I scrambled around to find a chair for her. I rolled out Jay's desk chair, and Beth perched on the edge as she began to fill out her admission form. She ran through all the usual questions: which medications he was taking, which appointments he'd been to, and which were coming up. She asked for a brief history of the previous few days and tapped the answers into her laptop.

"We'll be doing this every time, because you're likely to have visits from different nurses, depending on our schedules," she explained. "That way, each nurse will be able to see at a glance how William was doing the last time one of us visited."

He and I interrupted her simultaneously. "It's Jay."

Her face clouded over for a second before it cleared. "I get it," she hazarded. "It's your middle initial, right?"

"Exactly. My mother never liked the name William."

Beth's eyebrows rose a fraction. Jay was used to elaborating on this.

"I was named after my grandfather, William J. Wilson," he told her. "So I think I'm William J. Wilson II, or is it the third? Point is," he went on, "my mother agreed to that, but only if she could call me by my middle name, which was James. Somehow, that never caught on either, so I was always called Jay."

"It's no good referring to him as William," I added. "He won't answer to it."

Beth made a note. I had a fleeting vision of some medical person trying to rouse him when he was unconscious by calling him William and getting no response.

"Okay," said Beth. "By the way, the laptop is linked to Dartmouth, so they'll have this information right away. Have to say, we don't always get *their* records that fast."

She stood up, putting the computer out of harm's way on the chair, and took out her stethoscope, thermometer, and blood pressure equipment.

"I'm feeling great." Jay smiled at her. "My blood pressure's always perfect."

He'd been bragging about this for years, claiming it was due to his Scandinavian genes. It wasn't until I was dusting his dresser one day that I realized he was taking the same BP medication I was. He never bothered to ask his doctor what anything was for. If a doctor told him to do something, he did it—unless, of course, he didn't want to.

Giving up spirits, red wine, and spicy foods fell into this category, but he'd been ignoring that advice for a long time, and became used to paying the price with severe heartburn.

That was one reason it hadn't occurred to him his recent abdominal pain might herald something worse.

Beth took all his vitals anyway. "Now, let's take a look at this leg." She was using the cheerful sing-song voice nurses always seem to use, even in the worst circumstances. Jay winced as she unwrapped the three Ace bandages the surgical nurses had left around his calf and foot.

"They waste so much stuff," she muttered to herself. Followed by: "I don't think he needs quite this many. Two should do it."

After changing the dressing, asking me to pay attention since I might have to do it at some point, she looked up.

"Things are looking good." She gave us a reassuring smile as she reached for her bag. "See you on Friday."

❖ ❖ ❖

Thursday, September 4

Now that he was home from the hospital, I went down to the basement to find the walker from five years before, when Jay had flown off a snowmobile after a ride around the lake and broken his leg.

He did well, getting himself to the bathroom and back, relying on the walker. I would follow him in to make sure he didn't fall, since he was still taking fairly strong painkillers, and I worried about his balance. So far, he'd managed without my help.

After the nurse had gone, I left to run the usual errands, pick up the mail and buy something for lunch. When I returned, Jay told me he'd like to walk to the bathroom, so I handed him the walker and prepared to trail after him.

"I can do this on my own," he insisted. "You stay here, and I'll be back."

He sounded confident, so I busied myself checking his

emails while he made the trip down the passage leading to the bathroom. On his way back to bed, he called out.

As I ran down the corridor to help him, I glanced down at the floor and saw a trail of small dark-red spots on the pine floorboards. They were coming from one of the incisions on his leg.

"Jesus, Jayway," I said. "I think you've sprung a leak. She must not have done the dressing right. Let's get your leg elevated—that should help."

"Goddamn it." I heard his quick intake of breath as he spoke. "It hurts like hell when I put any weight on it."

He abandoned the walker and put his arm around my shoulders. Together we staggered back to bed, Jay gasping from time to time as he took his tentative steps.

"Sit here for a second." I lowered him, more clumsily than I intended, to the side of the bed. I pushed my bangs off my forehead. Helping him along had been hard work. Running for a towel to lay over the sheets, I helped him back in, and lifted his leg to place an extra pillow beneath it. He gave one more short gasp but didn't complain. I hoped that raising his leg would stop the bleeding, but I wasn't taking any chances. I called the VNA.

When I explained the situation, the dispatcher promised a call from Beth and a visit, should it be necessary.

"Oh, I think it will be necessary." I had to make her understand. "He's bleeding a lot."

"Just keep his leg elevated. Beth will call you as soon as she can."

Joyce, a tall nurse with an efficient but kindly way of doing things, showed up after I'd spoken to Beth, who was visiting a patient in Vermont. She, too, exclaimed at the view of the lake, took off her shoes, and followed me into the bedroom. She lost little time in gently unraveling the bandages to check on what was no longer an incision, but a wound in a noticeably swollen calf.

"It's rather pink," she said. "On a scale of one to ten..."

Jay interrupted her to say it didn't hurt much if he wasn't trying to walk.

She mopped the wound and changed the dressing, selecting the cleaner of the two Ace bandages.

She made a note. "I'll have them send some new ones. They'll be here tomorrow."

Leaving us with his leg elevated on a couple of pillows, and a few last words on pain management, she headed out of the door. The rest of the day passed uneventfully. Jay read and did a Sudoku puzzle, dozed, and ate some dinner.

But as the evening wore on, his pain became worse again, even if he didn't move at all. I was reluctant to give him too much medication, knowing it was morphine-based—and addictive. I'd seen the glaring headlines in the check-out line at the supermarket, detailing the latest celebrities to become its victims. I tried to ignore my fears as I gave him the maximum dose. It didn't seem to help. At least, not enough.

❊ ❊ ❊

Friday, September 5

After an almost sleepless night for both of us, I was hugely relieved when Beth called at seven-thirty the next morning to schedule a visit.

"Could you come sooner rather than later?" I asked, out of my husband's earshot. "I'm beginning to worry about this."

I imagine Beth assumed I was just one more nervous spouse, but she agreed to be with us by nine.

The meds had stopped working long before she arrived. After one look at Jay's face, pale with the effort of conquering the constant pain, Beth decided he needed to go to the hospital right away. The only question was whether he should return to Dartmouth or go to the local hospital first. There was no question in my mind.

"I don't think we should wait to deal with this." I saw only one option. "Besides, New London is so close." I gave Jay a hand with his clothes, then realized I had no way of getting him out of the house. We had no wheelchair. I made a note to get one by the end of the day.

"Got any ideas, Fred?" I was hopeful my creative engineer of a son would come up with a fix. He pointed at the rolling desk chair. We helped Jay sit on it and pushed him to the front door, maneuvering carefully through the awkward turn from our bedroom toward the hall.

I'd forgotten the two steps from the house to the driveway.

Fred, who often lifted weights while he watched TV, was impressively strong.

"I've got this." He lifted Jay with a grunt and carried him, step by slow step, out to the car. I could see sweat pouring off my son as he gritted his teeth and deposited Jay in the passenger seat, which I'd positioned as close as I could.

As I reached the *porte-cochere* outside the Emergency Room, a male nurse, alerted by a phone call from Beth, came out to meet us, pushing a wheelchair. Tall and spare, sporting a quarter-inch beard that was turning gray, he disappeared with my husband while I went to park somewhere legal.

As I walked back into the reception area, I wondered if Jay would be able to remember the sequence of events that had brought him here. I gave the receptionist his details, then asked to go back to see him, something I had done on every previous visit.

"Oh no," she announced. "They don't allow that."

"What do you mean? They always allow the next of kin in with a patient."

"They have to get him settled," said the deer-in-the-headlights girl behind the desk, staring at me through her glasses. "That's the rule."

This was nonsense. If I hadn't gone to park the car, I would have been with Jay now, as I had been the last time we were there, only days before.

I made a mental note of her name, Janice, and muttered something about dictatorships under my breath, but I waited, growing ever more anxious, for about five minutes before I approached her again. I got the same reply, and now Janice was looking nervously around, avoiding my eye. I guess she could tell I wasn't about to be trifled with.

I leaned across the desk, so there could be no mistake. "Right. I'm going back to see him, no matter what."

I walked to a different entrance, further down the corridor, and tried to open the door. It was locked, of course, but I could see the nurses' station, so I knocked quite firmly to attract their attention.

I got it.

The same male nurse appeared at the door and mouthed the words, "Go to the back entrance." I could see his name, Paul, embroidered on his uniform. I wouldn't forget it in a hurry. He had a scowl on his face now, but I didn't care as I sped around to the ambulance drop-off point. Paul met me in the unloading bay, with one of the EMTs in tow. He spread his arm wide as if to block my way.

"It's against the rules for you to go back there until the patient is settled."

I stared at him in disbelief. The EMT retreated, as if trying to make himself smaller.

"But this has never happened to me before." This was true. "I've always gone back with him." My voice was rising, and I could tell I was on the verge of tears. Two more nurses had appeared to see what the fracas was about and were standing behind Paul, looking at each other. I felt that even if they were on my side, they'd be obliged to show solidarity with another member of their team.

I couldn't hold back my sobs. "This is so unfair."

Paul remained impassive. A small, dark-haired woman, the hospital chaplain, eased her way between the nurses and came to stand next to me.

"Come with me." She led me through the back of the ER to the waiting room and sat me down, silently handing me some tissues. I found myself telling her, between sobs, about Jay's diagnosis, his embolism, his pain, and his upcoming cancer treatment.

"It's a lot." She reached for my hand.

Half an hour after we'd arrived, they let me in, much to Jay's relief, and mine. Still, the damage was done. I sat next to him as a nurse came in to check his vital signs. Apparently, they hadn't given him anything for pain yet.

"On a scale of one to ten..." the nurse began. It was the third time he'd been asked this today, and it wouldn't be the last.

"Nine," he gasped through clenched teeth.

"I'll be right back." She disappeared and returned almost immediately with a syringe of Dilaudid, which I'd never heard of. I would soon become familiar with this morphine-based painkiller, but right then, all I cared about was that Jay appeared to be relaxing, and the frown on his face was disappearing as I gazed at him.

"That's amazing stuff," I told the nurse, relieved.

She nodded. "It's very fast-acting. Although it wears off relatively fast too, so I'm going to recommend he go to Dartmouth-Hitchcock. They'll have to deal with the cause of this."

"So, should I get the car?" I asked.

"Sure, but your husband needs to go by ambulance. He's groggy, and besides, they'll handle him quicker that way."

❊ ❊ ❊

At Dartmouth Hospital they told us Jay needed to be admitted. "Unfortunately, this is what can happen when pain gets beyond a certain point," they informed us. "You must never let it get out of control again."

They didn't need to tell me that. Watching Jay in agony ratcheted up my own torture level to at least a seven.

He had to stay in for four days while they attempted to stave off his pain. They tried various remedies—a self-administered morphine pump, to begin with, coupled with some heavy-duty antibiotics for his infected leg. After a day or two, he felt more like himself. I sat by his bed, reading and writing in my journal, while he slept the sleep of a heavily drugged man. The wall clock seemed expressly designed to make time pass more slowly.

Over the weekend, a slim young doctor, her dark-blond hair dragged back into a ponytail, came in to change the dressing on his leg, asked about the pain level (now a four), and checked on his medications.

Standing with her back to the window, her face in shadow, she stuffed her stethoscope into the pocket of her jacket.

"You're going to have to learn to deal with pain," she began without any preamble or compassion. Her tone was that of an irritated schoolmistress rather than a concerned healer.

We gaped at her. We knew that. It's what we were trying to do. What was wrong with her? She continued to lecture us.

"Pancreatic cancer is the most painful of all the cancers, and there'll come a time when you'll have to choose between quantity and quality of life."

Jay gripped my hand. We'd been stunned into silence. Her remarks weren't news to us, but the way she made them was cool to the point of callous. She stood there, at the end of the bed, her lab coat open, obscuring the embroidered name on it.

My own pain level had suddenly risen to a ten. I could have hit her. I squeezed Jay's hand as hard as I could while I collected myself.

"What's your name?" I was having trouble keeping my voice steady.

"Claire Gaines."

I wouldn't forget it anytime soon.

"Do you work in the oncology department?" I continued.

"No, but I used to."

So, they threw you out, was what I wanted to say, because of your complete lack of empathy. Still, I was keenly aware I had to keep the medical personnel on our side. God knew what this woman might be capable of if we lost our cool with her.

So, I tried to hold my temper in check. I was more concerned with Jay's reaction. How dare she be so callous—so completely unaware of how a patient might be feeling?

"I think you've been particularly unhelpful and inappropriate," I said at last. "You can be sure I'll make everyone here aware of it."

Dr. Gaines gave me a blank stare as she turned and left the room.

We'd been aware, without discussing it, that deciding between quality and quantity of life might be a choice we'd have to make at some point but didn't need to be reminded of it right now. So, we certainly didn't need to be told about the pain. There was no one from palliative care to come and make the situation better—it was the weekend. At least I was with him. Someone needed to keep Jay's spirits up.

I made a decision. "I'm reporting her." And I did.

❋ ❋ ❋

Monday, September 8

Obviously, we couldn't take the morphine pump home with us, so they switched Jay to slow-release OxyContin tablets, and, in case that wasn't enough, Dilaudid if he needed it. Now that he was off the pump, he was beginning to feel anxious about how his pain would be managed. I worried about whether I'd get the doses and the timing of them right. There was so much to remember, and the consequences of a mistake might be irreversible.

They'd told us Jay's leg had to be raised at all times, and the pillows we'd been using to achieve this had been only partially successful. So, I sent Fred off to the nearest big town to order a bed with a head and foot that could be lifted using a remote.

Luckily, our king-sized bed consisted of two separate twins—we hadn't been able to maneuver anything bigger into the bedroom. The shop delivered the new one the next day, but replacing one half of our bed required building a new base for my side, which proved incredibly arduous. Fred persevered, and, sitting in the TV room, we could hear him sawing the supports to the right length and hammering them into place.

When he'd finished, a few hours later, my mattress was a couple of inches lower than Jay's. It didn't matter. We could still sleep together, which was all I cared about. Meanwhile, the raised foot of the bed made it easier to keep Jay's leg up while we waited for it to heal.

I wasn't sure I was ready to deal with the cancer team yet, but our first appointment was set for the following morning at nine. It would mean an early start.

Chapter 18
Meeting the Team

I had mixed feelings as I drove Jay to Dartmouth to meet the cancer team for the first time. I wished we didn't have to make this trip, but we had no choice if he was to survive. As I looked for a place to park the car, I wondered how I'd get him from the parking garage to the cancer center. Finding a spot for disabled motorists, I backed the car in and went to search for a wheelchair.

Several of them were huddled by the sliding doors of the hospital, but they were all extra-wide ones. Jay might have been more comfortable in one of those a few months ago. Now he was so much thinner, that my bag easily fitted in next to him.

I'd brought the white tote printed with bright-pink tea roses that I'd purchased in London because it held a lot. I was learning that every time we went to the hospital, they would give us a printout of what had transpired that day. So, I needed somewhere to stash that, as well as a bottle of water, Jay's newspapers, my tablet computer, and our phones.

We were supposed to check in by eight, and we arrived

in the parking garage with minutes to spare. By the time we got to the check-in desk, we were running late. Getting there had involved an elevator (too full of people to leave room for the wheelchair) and a walk that went on forever.

As we waited to sign in at reception, I checked out the waiting room. Apparently, someone had made an effort to make it look welcoming, almost informal. Recliner chairs (all occupied), comfortable armchairs, and sofas were arranged in casual groupings. Local newspapers, and magazines featuring beautiful people, lay on the coffee tables, and someone was carefully adding pieces to a jigsaw puzzle of the Eiffel Tower.

But the twenty-foot ceilings showed this was a hospital, and relaxation didn't come naturally. I guessed most of the people there were already in treatment and was encouraged to see that some appeared quite healthy, with good color, all their hair, and flesh on their bones.

Others were paper-thin, gaunt, and gray; some were bald, and some had their heads covered with hats or cleverly knotted scarves. One man wore a cowboy hat and would have looked carefree in any other environment. A basket of hand-crocheted ski hats, free for anyone who wanted one, sat on the bookcase, which displayed a depressing range of books about cancer.

I could recognize the carers, though. To the casual observer, they might have appeared like everyone else. Only they had a universally anxious expression and watched their patients closely. I was to become one of them.

A cheerful nurse led us to an examination room on the lower basement floor, where she took Jay's blood pressure and weighed him. I guessed they needed a baseline number, so they could monitor his weight as treatment progressed.

We waited. The room had no window and the fluorescent light made both of us appear ill. They'd tried to make it into a comfortable consulting room. Side by side on the loveseat, we marked time until our first appointment turned up. Jay tried to concentrate on his paper while I studied the posters on the wall, with their depictions of people's brightly colored organs.

I rose to get a cup of water from the sink in the corner, where a notice showed me how to wash my hands. I felt guilty as I ignored it and used a dab of sanitizer. Soon the members of the cancer team began to trickle in, some with a student in tow.

Donna Santoro introduced the pain specialist from the palliative care department. A young and slender nutritionist, Jeannette, who I decided could have used a square meal herself, came to talk about eating small meals regularly throughout the day. Still, they weren't really the people we wanted to see.

Where was the doctor?

A quick knock on the door heralded his arrival. He turned out to be in his forties, tanned with black hair that had a tendency to stand on end. He wore black-framed spectacles and a bow tie, which made him resemble a Norman Rockwell painting of a little boy pretending to be a doctor. He strode in and shook Jay's hand, then mine, with a firm grip that inspired confidence.

After apologizing for his lateness, he introduced himself as Dr. Petrakis, head of the pancreatic cancer unit.

"I'm here to answer all your questions," he said. "Feel free to ask me anything."

Jay began by grilling him about his qualifications. "How long have you been here?"

"Seven years."

"Where did you get your degree?"

"Columbia."

My spouse was a Yale man, which gave him a baseless mistrust of other Ivy Leaguers—but he took this piece of news on the chin. After all, he was sitting in the Dartmouth University hospital, and couldn't afford to antagonize the medical staff.

"What's your experience with this type of cancer?"

Dr. Petrakis answered everything with patience and good humor, something we would find with almost everyone at that hospital.

When Jay had finished the job interview, he got to the point. "Okay," he said. "What's my situation?"

I'd brought a notebook with me to record everything, but was finding it difficult to concentrate on listening and writing at the same time. Soon, I put down my pen and laid the notebook on my lap. It would be more important to hear what they were saying, I thought.

"What do you know right now?" Dr. Petrakis asked.

"Well, I've got pancrea..." He stumbled over the word. "Cancer. I need to know what can be done about it."

"Of course. Let me explain what we're talking about here."

The oncologist picked up a green marker and began to draw on a whiteboard. "This is your pancreas." He circled it on the board. "It's right here, next to your stomach and your liver. It helps digestion and maintains the right sugar levels in the blood."

I saw Jay watching the marker as it illustrated his insides.

"Your tumor is roughly here." Dr. Petrakis drew another emerald circle on the board. "It's not very big, and as far as we can tell, it hasn't spread, which is good."

"So, can you operate?" My husband always preferred a straightforward solution.

"Even though it's not so large, we would like to try and shrink it before we consider surgery. We would use radiation, primarily, with some chemotherapy as an adjunct treatment."

Jay was silent as he thought this over. I was feeling numb as I listened. At that moment, we were joined by another man in a white coat.

"This is Dr. Abboud," said Dr. Petrakis. "He's in charge of our radiation unit. You'll be seeing quite a bit of him, I think. Right, Doctor?"

After shaking hands, Dr. Abboud leaned back against the wall and explained the plan—radiation five times a week for six weeks.

"We will set an aggressive plan of treatment," he reassured us, "At the end of that, we'll re-evaluate and see what we can do next."

I thought Jay was looking intimidated by the prospect of having to be here every day. He raised his head and glanced at one doctor, then the other. "Let's cut to the chase," he said. "What are my chances of survival?"

I didn't want to hear the answer.

Dr. Petrakis sat down on a stool near us and swiveled gently as he talked. I couldn't take my eyes off him. This was my life he was talking about, too.

"There are people who can live for five years, sometimes longer." He looked at Jay. "They tend to be people whose cancer hasn't metastasized, those who are candidates for an operation that successfully removes the tumor."

I was trying to work out exactly what this meant. They had no way of knowing—that was the bottom line. Then Jay spoke.

"How long if I do nothing?" he asked. Why was that even a question? It was ridiculous. He was going to have treatment, no question.

"Typically, without any medical interventions, a person might live from between four and a half months to conceivably twice as long." God, this man was precise. I guess that was good in a radiation specialist.

"When do we start?"

❀ ❀ ❀

On the way home in the car, I let Jay talk. Although we'd both listened to identical words, we seemed to have heard completely different things.

Jay was heartened by the meeting—what he heard was the miracles part. He was buoyed by the fact that Dr. Petrakis wasn't discounting surgery.

"Miracles happen—isn't that what he told us?"

"He did. You never know." I gripped the steering wheel to make myself concentrate on the road, not on my thoughts.

"They'll do the surgery once the tumor is smaller, so that sounds promising."

"Yes, it does."

"They told us it hasn't spread." Jay wanted to reassure me—and maybe himself.

"Which is a huge plus, because it means the radiation can do most of the work." I needed to encourage him, mistakenly believing this would be a less debilitating option than chemo.

"I could live for at least five years."

"Also, the longer you can keep going, the more time there is for them to make new discoveries." I laid a hand over Jay's.

❄ ❄ ❄

I'd heard something very different in that meeting.

Without surgery, life might be prolonged, but the tumor couldn't be cured. It was clinging to the celiac and splenic arteries, so would probably never be operable. The doctors used words like resecting instead of operating, perhaps hoping we wouldn't catch its meaning, but I understood. What I heard and hadn't taken into consideration before, was that Jay had atrial fibrillation and COPD (another name for emphysema, though mild). These conditions would make him an unlikely candidate for surgery, even if the radiation and chemo reduced the size of the tumor.

Without treatment, he would last four and a half months. With chemo and radiation, it should be longer. Without an operation, though, it would be a miracle if he made it to five years. The whole thing was a crapshoot. It always was. There was no point in thinking about it. We would have to take life and love one day at a time from now on.

Meanwhile, his treatment was bound to be exhausting. For both of us.

Chapter 19
Treatment

The schedule was to consist of daily radiation with chemo added on Mondays and Thursdays. Once a week, starting at the end of September, we would meet, one by one, with each member of the oncology team. Sometimes we'd also have to go to the surgical department so they could check on the progress of Jay's leg. These appointments might total five or six a day. This timetable would run for four weeks, so my calendar was a mass of appointments. I could hardly wait for Halloween, when the horror would all be over.

Traveling to Dartmouth-Hitchcock every day had one attraction: the late-September scenery was wonderful. We would drive north on I-89 with the early morning sun at our backs. The curving highway wound between hills covered with pine and birch forests, passing farms and a small ski resort, but otherwise without any sign of human life.

During the second week of Jay's regimen, in late September, we drove around a bend in the road and were caught unawares by the sight of trees newly aflame with color, seemingly overnight. I was so surprised that I pulled over to give us a chance to take it all in.

"It's gorgeous, isn't it?" I said.

He smiled at me. "Sure is." He covered my hand with his.

* * *

Jay was paying for a lifetime with no morning-after effects by nursing the mother of all hangovers following each of his radiology appointments.

"God, I hope it's worth it," he muttered. "I'd much rather be going to Montreal with the Sargents."

Since we hadn't been able to go to Montana to see our old friends, we'd planned to meet them in Canada, only three hours away by car, where, in spite of, or perhaps because of, her terminal cancer, they'd be embarking on an autumn cruise.

"We'll go another time." I hoped it was true, but it sounded like bravado, even to me.

* * *

Before each chemo session, they took blood and tested it to determine the chemical formula they would give him. This depended on the white cell count, among other things. After stopping at what my husband cordially referred to as the Vampire Room, we'd have to sit and wait until someone came to escort us from the oncology waiting room to the infusion unit.

That sounded mild enough. Like the sort of place where you could let tea steep until it's infused into the water, before sipping its life-giving qualities. Not literally life-giving, obviously, but at least providing the mental vitamins called energy and hope.

On the first day, Jay's reclining armchair was wedged into the corner in a tiny cupboard of a room, with another chair next to it and a small side table in between.

The first thing to strike me was the dim light since the room had no window. The wall with the door was made of glass, with a privacy curtain half drawn across. I felt sure that with it closed, the cubicle would be even darker and more depressing. A plastic holder opposite offered a brochure called *Chemotherapy and You*, *People* magazine, and *Sports Illustrated*, thereby, no doubt, covering all the possible interests of the patients.

A week later, with Jay feeling nauseous before we even started, I prayed he'd be assigned somewhere he'd be able at least to have a window. Walking toward us, I could see a chunky male nurse with round glasses. I noted the name Brian on his scrubs.

"Which one's the patient?" he quipped. This joke was so unexpected that I didn't get it right away. I must have looked dazed because he took the handles of the chair from me, quite gently, and began to push Jay into the center of the building again.

"Please." I put a hand on the arm pushing the wheelchair. "Could he possibly have a spot with a window?"

Brian paused, then apparently caught the eye of a senior nurse coming the other way.

"Any chance of a window room for this fine gentleman?"

She barely broke stride. "I think 4B might be free now."

I heaved a sigh of relief. As I saw it, anything I could do to make this more bearable for us both was a plus.

The room turned out to be a private one, with a bed, which faced away from the window and toward the corridor, but at least there was daylight. Brian bustled around, helping Jay take off his shoes, finding a warm blanket for him, and generally making him feel cozy. This was more like it, I thought.

To one side stood the pole on which the bag of poison would be hung as it drip, drip, dripped into the back of Jay's hand.

Brian inserted a cannula—a fancy name I'd learned for the tube where the drugs go in. I was doing so well with the medical terminology by then that I was often asked whether I was a member of the medical profession.

"Your mixture will be here as soon as it comes down from the lab," Brian said.

Jay's eyes were closed, but he nodded wearily. My mind wandered as I imagined, not for the first time, a dark basement where white-coated men, eyes a bit crazed and hair awry, were pouring purple and green fluids into a test tube and waiting for a few sparks and a cloud of noxious vapor to emerge from the top.

"It's ready for Mr. Wilson," they would say, handing it over to the messenger. He would speed along the corridors and up the stairs. Oh, no. Wait. More likely, he'd saunter, one hand in his pocket, stopping to chat to the comely receptionist outside the cancer center. Otherwise, he'd be here by now, wouldn't he?

I noticed I was tapping my foot and forced myself to stop.

After a while, a tall female nurse, wearing a smile and scrubs dotted with pink and yellow teddy bears, walked into the room, a couple of bags of crystal-clear liquid in one hand. Her cheery bears were hardly discernible behind an almost transparent robe that enveloped her, and she was sporting purple disposable gloves, a cap to cover her hair, and a face mask. This was hanging around her neck, as though she'd forgotten to put it on. If I needed any further proof that chemotherapy drugs were dangerous, this hazmat gear was it.

She was followed by a nurse who'd been seeing to patients on the other side of the starkly lit corridor. Her only protection was a disposable plastic apron. Putting on her glasses, the tall one hung the bags on the pole and began reading a series of letters and numbers from each, while the second checked them against the computer printout in her hand. The only words I could make out were Jay's name and birth date.

"That looks like more than he got last time," I commented, wondering how long it would take to get this much liquid into his system when it was only dripping in.

"Dr. Petrakis asked us to give your husband a liter of fluids. He's dehydrated, which is contributing to his tiredness."

"Oh, good." I made a note to Google the effects of dehydration on a person. Could it be that some symptom I was putting down to the disease was being caused by lack of fluids? "And how long...?"

"About two hours."

I began to be concerned. "Jay has radiation at four. I think it's their last appointment of the day."

I thought he might be happy to skip it for once. He found it exhausting, but knowing his life depended on it, he slogged on through the treatments.

"Don't worry. We'll make sure he makes it."

I needed an infusion myself, I realized. I hadn't eaten anything since breakfast, and it was after two now.

"Darling," I said, when Jay was settled with his drip and a newspaper to hand. "If you don't mind, I'm going to get something to eat." Belatedly, I remembered he hadn't had anything either. "Can I get you something?"

"I don't think so..."

"How about an Italian ice? It's nice and cool. It'll be refreshing."

"Okay," he agreed, but I could tell he didn't really care. I leaned over to kiss his forehead. "Back in a minute."

He was asleep when I returned, and I left the lemon ice to melt while I went off for soup and a breadstick at the hospital café. That cashier thought I was a member of staff too, because I showed up so regularly.

We made it to radiology with seconds to spare, where the team of friendly young radiologists asked him about his weekend as they wheeled him away for another silent assault on his body.

I made a cup of coffee from the machine provided for carers and sat down to wait, pulling my tablet from my bag and logging onto Dartmouth-Hitchcock's Wi-Fi. Even my computer thought I worked there. Every morning, it told me how long my commute would take that day. If only it could have answered the really important questions I had. But those were questions no one was prepared to answer.

❊ ❊ ❊

We were about halfway through the treatments, with only another three weeks to go. The hematologist had taken blood samples a couple of hours before, and we'd been waiting to be told what effect the results would have on the chemical cocktail Jay was having that afternoon. I managed to find an empty reclining chair for him to stretch out on while he waited, and he was dozing. I was hoping he would feel a bit better, a bit stronger, by the time I woke him.

When I did, I could tell the nap hadn't helped. I planted myself in front of him, to give him something solid to hang on to while he stood up. I found it hard, sometimes, staying solid.

I pushed him in his wheelchair from the cancer center waiting area toward the doors of the infusion unit, which opened towards us, ready to send us flying if we didn't slow down. As we entered, I glanced to the right at the nurses' station, and Brian walked over to help.

"Follow me," he said. Then to Jay: "We've got a nice bed for you today."

I was grateful Jay might have a chance to rest, perhaps sleep, for a while. He was weak from his intense treatment schedule. It definitely wasn't making him feel better. If anything, he was sicker than before. His weight was down to 170.

And his nausea was still debilitating. The doctors were scratching their heads over him.

"Oh," decided Chemotherapy guy, "it's not the chemo causing it—it's the radiation."

"Nonsense." Radiation guy's rebuttal was firm. "It's the chemo."

I'd begun to think of them as the one with the weed killer and the one with the flamethrower. Jay liked these metaphors—I think it reflected something of how he felt at the end of treatment days.

Still, they were trying different anti-nausea medications each time he came to the hospital.

"The goal is to keep you pain and nausea-free without making you drowsy all the time."

"Sounds good." I heard some skepticism in my husband's voice.

"It's been..." Dr. Petrakis consulted Jay's notes on his laptop. "Three weeks since your operation. Your wife tells me you can put a little weight on that leg."

"I can manage a few steps with a walker, but I need to be awake for that, right?" He didn't mention that the 'few steps' were only from the bed to the wheelchair.

The doctor smiled. "Yep, awake would help," he said. "These meds should allow you to do that."

At least, I reflected, with the pain more manageable, we would be making progress. The cancer medications were lowering Jay's ability to fight infections, so I hoped the leg wound would be healed completely before his immune system became too compromised. It would still bleed occasionally for no reason I could discern. Still, the visiting nurses didn't seem too concerned about it, so I tried not to worry either.

By now, it seemed the nurses were beginning to worry about me. I found it increasingly difficult to find time to take care of myself. I did my best to look as attractive as I could, but there simply wasn't time for anything beyond the essentials. My wardrobe had become more of a uniform than an exercise in dressing. Jeans and sweaters formed the basis of it, and I made sure everything was washable at home.

My makeup had dwindled to a thin layer of moisturizer to protect my face from the wind, and a dab of lipstick, since it was the one thing Jay commented on if I wasn't wearing it. Why bother to emphasize my eyes with liner and mascara when they had natural shadows around them now?

In Connecticut, I used to have an occasional massage or manicure, go for a walk, or meet my friends for coffee or a movie. I didn't have the same opportunities here, because I was spending all my time with Jay. Once, knowing he would be supervised in the infusion unit, I booked a massage at a beauty parlor nearby. It ought to have helped me relax, but I don't think it succeeded. I thought I would never relax again.

Sometimes all I wanted was a hot cup of tea, yet it seemed as though the second I took a minute to prepare one, Jay would need something. He wanted me to open or close the blinds, or bring him some milk/apple juice/beef broth/his razor/the commode/the newspaper/a pill/a towel/clean sheets and on and on.

So, cups of tea went unfinished. Meals were nonexistent. I ate snacks all day—nuts, soup, asiago breadsticks from the hospital café, fruit, yogurt, and popcorn. When the children came to visit, they'd cook for us, hoping their dad would eat something they'd made. If he didn't want it that day, I lied, saying he was bound to feel like it the next.

Bertie made pasta with homemade vegetarian vodka sauce. I never thought I'd consume vodka, but I loved it and asked him for the recipe. Jay only managed a spoonful before abandoning it.

When I did manage to leave the house by myself, I could only spare an hour at most, in case Jay needed something. I went to the bank, picked up the mail from our post office box, shopped for groceries, and of course, visited the local pharmacy practically daily. The staff knew me well by now. Especially the pharmacists, whose grave smiles as each new prescription was ordered, stoked my fear that I could expect no positive outcome.

I thought longingly of my friends in Fairfield, many of whom knew little of what was keeping me away. I didn't want too much sympathy—it only made me feel sorry for myself. In New London, everyone asked after my husband and wanted to sympathize. I kept my answers brief, so I wouldn't start crying.

I preferred errands that brought me into contact with people who knew nothing of what was going on. I didn't mind dropping off books for the library's book sale, taking old fireworks to the fire station, or going to the dump.

But these domestic sorties soon became hard to schedule, as Jay required more attention. Having discovered my predicament, the palliative care coordinator told me I could arrange for someone to come in and be with him while I did something just for me. These assistants could be booked via the VNA.

They weren't a huge success. Jay grumbled about them, and I felt guilty for leaving him with someone he considered too inexperienced, too rough while adjusting his bedclothes, a smoker... Often he'd doze, or pretend to, until I came back.

But I needed that time off so, even though they were expensive, I used their services. I would go for a manicure or a walk, get the snow tires put on the car, or drive forty minutes to the mall to distract myself with window shopping. I rarely bought anything.

This kind of help would be free once he was officially designated a hospice patient, but he wasn't at that point yet. Nor did I want him to be, because it would mean hope was gone.

While he slept, I could write, and writing helped. I'd sit in Jay's Windsor chair at the head of the pine dinner table we'd bought ourselves as a wedding present thirty years before, staring out of the picture window at the lake. On rainy days, the whole landscape was painted in varying shades of gray, a light mist obscuring any hills I might normally see. I'd listen to the calming beat of the clock, made by a quirky artist from an old pump of some sort, ticking in the hall.

❋ ❋ ❋

At the end of October, after six weeks of treatments, we got paroled. A whole month, during which all we had to do was show up every so often to prove the patient was doing fine. Then, around Thanksgiving week, they would give him another CT scan and decide what to do next.

I rejoiced that we wouldn't have to make the exhausting commute every day, and we might have time to take a drive, perhaps in the opposite direction, just for the hell of it. It was something encouraging to contemplate.

And maybe Jay would begin to eat again.

Chapter 20
Weed

Late October

For years, I tried to cook things Jay enjoyed. If the results weren't always stellar, I improvised. I would sometimes serve him overdone roast beef and tell him it was pot roast. He ate it. I would make an effort to lay the table properly and find him a napkin or a paper towel—he must have gone through a forest of trees in napkins alone.

Shortly after we bought our first microwave, he decided to diet, and we made fat-free popcorn every night instead of eating dinner. In fact, it was the only thing we knew how to make in that giant black box that sat cluttering up the kitchen counter.

When the boys arrived to live with us after Susan died, they were five and eight, and they needed British comfort food—shepherd's pie, Irish stew, and rice pudding. Jay gamely ate along. For years.

Then he got sick and eating became painful.

"Worst idea for a diet you've ever had," said Fred, trying to lighten the mood.

* * *

Before his diagnosis, Jay had been quite robust. Since our trip to Russia, he'd lost a few pounds around his middle, which made him look fitter than he'd been for a long time. He managed to get into shorts he hadn't worn for years and was pleased that, almost effortlessly, he was succeeding in losing weight.

"I'm aiming for 190 pounds," he announced in June. A doctor had once told him he ought to weigh the same as he did in college if he wanted to stay well, but he'd been stuck between 205 and 215 for ages. "Only another five to go."

Now, neither of us mentioned that he was fading away because he was eating so little due to the pain in his stomach. For a month or two, while he waited for successive test results, he carried on with his morning routine. After breakfast, he'd head off to Jake's, the small convenience store at the local gas station, to buy his newspapers and coffee.

I tried to get him to brew and drink it at home, but I think he liked those little trips into the world. The employees greeted him as if they hadn't seen him for days. Pete, the lanky aging hippie behind the cash register, whose life had clearly taken some difficult detours before depositing him there, always had Jay's papers ready.

When his treatment started in September, our appointments were at eight each morning, which meant we had to leave the house by seven-thirty. This was much too early for me to eat anything, but Jay would unfailingly break his fast about thirty minutes after getting out of bed, no matter what the hour.

Although he managed to get himself up and dressed, he had no time to sit and eat, so he would slide into the passenger seat of the car and ease his injured leg in, while I juggled a banana and his slice of crumb cake. As often as not, he'd be holding three strips of bacon between his teeth, ready to breakfast en route.

For the first week or so of his treatment, I would stop

at Jake's on the way. Pete would ask after him and I would answer with something designed to encourage me as much as him. When Jay began skipping solid food, I started to sweeten his coffee with real sugar to add calories.

Jeannette, the attractive, slim nutritionist on the oncology team, was supposed to make sure patients didn't lose weight. When it became obvious Jay was having trouble with his appetite, she suggested ways of taking in smaller amounts more frequently. She offered us ready-made "foods"—prepackaged mixes to make milkshakes, and breakfast bars, made from shredded cardboard, according to my husband. The shakes languished in the kitchen cabinet, alongside the bars, so I called Jeannette.

"He doesn't mind my vanilla protein shake." I was talking about the one I often made in the summer to provide me with a quick meal on the go. "But I don't think it has enough protein, and I remember your saying he needed it. He's not eating very much else, as you know."

"I'll give you some samples of a high-protein shake—it comes in chicken and beef broth, too. Twenty grams per cup."

This sounded more promising. I was beginning the long journey of subterfuge when it came to his nutrition—trying to sneak in extra calories and protein if I possibly could. He quite liked the shake, especially when I added half a banana as I whizzed it up with some crushed ice. He would carry it, in a tall beaker with a straw, to drink in the car on the way to the hospital, which meant that he stopped drinking coffee, almost without realizing it.

I tried to get Jay to taste the protein-rich beef drink, but it turned out to be something like a hot milkshake in consistency, and he only sipped his way through half a cup before giving up on it. The remaining eleven envelopes joined the other supplements in the cabinet.

"Have we got any proper beef broth?" he asked.

I hunted through my old cookbooks in the pantry and

discovered the one that had come free with my mother's new gas stove in the fifties. It contained simple-to-make recipes for unsophisticated foods. My mother's recipes, written on old envelopes or slips of paper with occasional buttery thumbprints on them, were leafed into the pages.

I found the recipe for beef broth—it consisted of some bones, roasted in the oven with carrots, onions, and celery, and then boiled for several hours. A glass of sherry was an optional addition. I thought Jay might prefer the flavor of red wine and hoped it would evaporate in the cooking. I was so happy to have him back, now that he wasn't drinking alcohol anymore, that I didn't want to jinx it by giving it to him inadvertently.

Jay would manage almost a cup of broth at a time, which I'd serve him in a small mug—the amount appeared less intimidating. Sometimes, I could persuade him to have some buttered toast, cut into thin strips, with it.

He would make more of an effort over dinner, which might be a minimal piece of fish or some stew, with potatoes and perhaps a small portion of broccoli or salad. He seldom finished the child-sized portions I gave him, even though he'd been brought up as a member of the Clean Plate Club. To encourage him, I'd bought some smaller dishes, so the food wouldn't look lonely, as it did on our dinner plates.

His tastes were changing, too. I noticed that what he really felt inclined to eat, albeit in tiny portions, was the comfort food of his childhood. Occasionally, I could tempt him with a chocolate chip cookie, which I baked at home, hoping the smell wafting through from the kitchen might make him feel hungry.

But he continued to get thinner and weaker, and we still had some weeks of treatment to go. Even when it ended, Jay didn't feel any better, and I thought he was becoming discouraged. His beard started to grow because he couldn't be bothered to shave. He wasn't interested in talking to any of the children or watching a movie. He'd read a page or two of the paper and let it fall to the floor. He had begun taking an anti-anxiety pill, though it didn't appear to help.

And he still wasn't eating.

I felt helpless and was getting desperate, because his calorie intake was so low. No matter what I cooked to try and tempt him, he would only take a mouthful or two to please me before shaking his head.

Looking at him as he lay on our bed, I could see his breastbone, always somewhat prominent, like the peaks of a mountain range, above his abdomen, which fell away to a valley below his ribs. I hadn't ever seen his hip bones before. He weighed 157 pounds.

"Don't lose any more weight." I tried to smile. "Or you'll be lighter than I am." And I'm eight inches shorter than you, I thought. I didn't have to say it aloud. Jay understood.

✳ ✳ ✳

Throughout his illness, nurses we met would refer casually to "the new normal." They'd used the expression when he could no longer walk unaided, and again when he began to spend almost all his time in bed. I was sick of the new normal. Jay's weight was fading so fast he looked worse than anorexic to me. Yet the only thing the doctors at Dartmouth were doing was prescribing more anti-nausea tablets, none of which revived his appetite.

My daughter, Helenka, had contacts in Colorado, where marijuana had recently been made legal. We both knew it was supposed to make people hungry.

"What do you think, Jay?" she asked when she came to visit. Her eyes betrayed her concern, though she kept her voice light. "Ready to try a little weed?"

"Why not?" He shrugged. "Nothing else seems to be working." He gave her a crooked grin.

Back in the living room, where all the discussions I didn't want him to hear took place, I grilled Helenka. "I don't think he should be smoking," I said. "He's got that stuff he hacks up and can't get rid of. He keeps clearing his throat, which tires him out, and I'd hate it to get worse."

"Stop looking so worried, Ma. Let me get you some tea." She knew this constituted my miracle cure for everything. As she switched on the electric kettle and threw a teabag into the red mug saying *Keep Calm and Carry On,* she began to tell me what the options were.

"There are these shops where you can buy a special pipe for vaping." Seeing my blank expression, she carried on. "The thingy looks a bit like my fake cigarette." I was familiar with this. Helenka had given up smoking a while ago, but still took a hit of nicotine from a slender black tube that glowed blue at one end when she drew on it, but gave off no smoke, only a breath of odorless steam.

I must still have looked dubious.

"They don't smell, either," she reassured me. "So, the nurses won't know."

I hadn't considered this, and in any case, didn't care what anyone thought, now.

"We could try other things, too. How about some Alice B. Toklas brownies?"

These were brownies containing pot, which I'd heard worked faster taken that way. They might be easier for Jay to deal with.

"Where on earth will you find those?"

"I can make them with some marijuana butter. I'll get my friends to send some from Colorado."

Thank goodness for my free-spirited daughter.

"Could you make chocolate chip cookies?" I said. "They're his favorite."

❖ ❖ ❖

I kept them in a plastic container in Jay's nightstand. Every time I opened the drawer, the intense aroma of illicit plants would waft out, betraying the contents. It wasn't a smell I particularly liked, but Jay would eat a small cookie once a day, and with a mischievous air, began to tell friends he was now a pothead. This, coming from a man who'd been against recreational drugs all his adult life, showed me his sense of humor was still intact.

But it still wasn't enough to make him eat.

Chapter 21
Failure to Thrive

A few days before Jay's final treatment, I was Googling pancreatic cancer, looking for the statistics about how long people could survive. They called them survival statistics, but of course, since everyone is mortal and, in the end, succumbs to something, they meant delayed death statistics.

I don't know what was propelling me to do it because the news was never encouraging, but I had the feeling that with enough information, I could somehow make things better. As I scrolled down the screen, I noticed something about Steve Jobs, one of the founders of Apple Inc., and the fact that he'd survived with pancreatic cancer for seven years. I clicked through. Anything that might give me hope was a good thing.

As I read the article, I looked up the medical words I didn't understand. There was one word, cachexia, which I'd never heard. Next to it was a picture of an emaciated Steve Jobs. I read on.

Cachexia was an extreme form of involuntary weight loss, often seen in cancer patients and, in many cases, the actual cause of death. Sitting at Jay's desk in the darkened bedroom, with only the glow of the computer screen for illumination, I felt a shiver run through me, despite the warmth of the room.

This must be what was happening to my husband. He was literally starving to death. Why hadn't the doctors noticed? It was all very well for the nutritionist, Jeannette, to recommend small meals and bites of this and that, but could they not see what was going on? I dashed at my cheeks with the back of my hand and pressed my lips together as tears of helplessness began to run down my face. I took a breath. I couldn't allow Jay simply to waste away. I would have to do something.

The following day, at our weekly meeting with the specialists, it was clear Jay was in trouble. He weighed 155 pounds. I stared at the nurse, whose job it was to record this disaster.

"Fred told me this was the worst diet ever. I guess he's right." As Jay smiled, I could see the muscles of his face moving beneath the skin.

The nurse and I helped him onto the examination table and found him a couple of pillows and some warm blankets. He dozed—there was no telling how long we might have to wait. I didn't resent the occasionally poor timekeeping of the doctors. After all, they sometimes spent longer than the allotted time with us when we needed to talk.

The medical staff streamed in and out. The nutritionist. The palliative care doctor. And Dr. Petrakis, who went through a series of questions and listened as Jay described his debilitating nausea.

The doctor checked all the current medications and prescribed a new one to be added intravenously with the chemo scheduled next. We were almost at the end of the course of treatment, thank God.

I was aware the strain was beginning to tell on me. While Jay was undergoing that day's dose of therapy, I held onto my feelings so resolutely that my whole body was tense. Something had to give.

But I couldn't find anywhere in the cancer center for a person who needed to have a meltdown. The waiting room was full of other patients, and I didn't want the sympathy of strangers. I drifted blindly into one of the hospital's huge hallways and came across a hard bench to sit on. There was no point in trying to control my tears any longer.

"Is everything all right?" I looked up with blurry eyes, to see the young intern from the palliative care department, who'd noticed me in passing and walked over. I wondered, as I often did, why people asked, when it was so apparent everything was not all right.

I had to make someone listen. "I think Jay's cachectic."

He raised an eyebrow. "What makes you think so?"

"Look at him!" I burst out. "He's six foot two, and he weighs 155 pounds. You can see every single one of his ribs." I started to cry again, and fished in my handbag for the small box of tissues one of the nurses had handed me a couple of weeks ago. They weren't much use, but I managed to blow my nose.

"I'm sorry," I explained. "But I don't think he's going to die of cancer. He's going to die of starvation." I could hear myself beginning to sound hysterical.

The intern sat down next to me. "Have you eaten?"

"What? No. I mean..."

"You need to keep your strength up. I'm not sure you're right about this, but I'll ask Dr. Petrakis to come and talk to you. It might take a while. He's still seeing patients."

"Thank you." I was profoundly grateful. I needed to be heard by someone who understood.

"Now go and get yourself a bowl of soup. You've got time."

I bought a packet of nuts and returned to the bench, where Dr. Petrakis found me half an hour later. His hair was refusing to lie flat, and his bow tie was a tad askew, but he sat by me and took my hand.

"I know you're worried," he began. "You've been

amazing, and this is a lot to deal with."

I nodded and removed my hand to find another tissue.

"I think we'd like to keep your husband in overnight," he told me. "We can give him some intravenous nutrition, and that should help."

I turned to face him. "Intravenous nutrition?"

"Yes. It's an effective way to get some calories into him without the nausea being an issue."

I couldn't imagine how food could be delivered into Jay's veins, but I didn't care. If the doctor believed this would work, I'd take it.

"Thank God," I said, and burst into tears again.

✱ ✱ ✱

Jay stayed in over the weekend. They put a needle in his arm and hooked it up to a three-liter bag containing something that resembled milk. Just until his appetite comes back, they explained. To my relief, he was looking more alert when I came in the next morning.

"Got the papers?" he asked. I laughed shakily.

"Good morning to you, too," I said. "Of *course* I have them. I wouldn't dare arrive without your newspapers."

He had barely managed a glance at the photos and a quick read of the football scores recently, so this interest was a wonderful sign.

I leaned over and kissed him, avoiding the tube that was pumping the white fluid into his right arm.

"They're going to come and weigh me again when this is done," he told me. "Apparently, I can be weighed in the bed, so I don't even have to get up."

I felt my shoulders relax for the first time in days. "We'll have you home in no time."

"They're saying I can go home tomorrow."

"Wonderful." I sighed with relief. "I think the girls

might be coming up to see you."

Jay brightened. "That's great."

It was fortunate that they came to visit him, because they managed to distract him from the fact that the young doctor who was keeping an eye on Jay was reluctant to let him leave the hospital.

"How's the nausea?" he asked.

"Well, it's still there, but I feel like I have a bit more energy."

"It's clear you're feeling better," the doctor said. "But that won't last unless you keep getting the TPN—the intravenous nutrition. We need to figure out a way for you to do that. So, I want Dr. Petrakis to sign you out."

"And when will that be?" My frustrated husband sounded as though he were talking through clenched teeth. I felt my shoulders tense for a second, but part of me thought this was positive, too. He hadn't had the energy to lose his temper for quite a while. But if he needed more nutrition and each bag of "food" took twelve hours, how was he going to get it if he was at home?

"I am not waiting till Monday."

I recognized that stubborn voice.

"Let me see what I can do," said the doctor, who'd taken a step back at his patient's tone.

What he did was to arrange for the TPN to be delivered to the house, where I would administer it daily.

The milky liquid, labeled "Specially mixed for William J. Wilson," arrived in chilled Styrofoam containers each week, along with vials of supplements that had to be added to the "milk" just before I connected Jay to it. A week's supply took up both vegetable drawers in the bottom of the fridge. The hospital had put in an order for a pump, pre-set to the speed of drip required, as well as all kinds of other impedimenta that I would have to use.

For the first day or two after Jay's return home I refused to do it. I was terrified of making a mistake and doing him some real damage. I begged Joan, a no-nonsense nurse, to handle it for me.

But on the third day, she told me I'd have to do it myself. She'd demonstrated how it worked and made me watch her over the previous couple of days, and now she was ready to hand the treatment over to me. "Tell you what. You do it, and I'll keep an eye on you all the way through, so you have backup."

A five-page list of instructions had arrived with the supplies, so I focused on the first page. I'd already washed my hands and used a dollop of antiseptic gel for good measure. I checked off item one. Jay dozed, seemingly oblivious to what we were doing.

Joan spoke in a stage whisper. "You took the bag out of the fridge an hour ago, didn't you?"

"Yes."

It was lying on the bedside table and she placed a hand on it to check the temperature. She didn't want me to put ice-cold liquid into Jay's veins. "That seems about right. Okay. Now what?"

I read from the page. "Gather supplies. One coil of tubing." This was a clear plastic disposable tube, and I had a box of them behind the armchair, where I was storing as many medical items as I could, to preserve the impression Jay was in a normal bedroom. I took it out of its plastic bag and put it next to the milk.

"Two syringes—one with the Heparin. One with saline in it, to flush the line." These were pre-filled, and I'd laid them alongside the bag. They were important to make sure the little tube in Jay's upper arm was clean, and no blood clot formed to block it during the infusion.

"Two alcohol swabs." I had a whole container of these and fished out a couple. "And two batteries." I considered it a waste to use two new nine-volt batteries every day, but they ensured nothing failed in the middle of the infusion.

"You forgot the syringes for the additives and vitamins," Joan said.

I checked the list again. She was right. Well, of *course* she was.

"But you have the vitamins and TPN additives out. Good." She glanced at Jay, who was lying silent, his eyes closed. "I'll watch while you add them to the big bag. It's not difficult, don't worry."

I took the cap off a small sterile syringe and laid it on a clean paper towel. Then I pried the lid off the two small vials. Under the lids, the vials were sealed but a needle could penetrate to the contents. I took another look at the instructions. I was only on page 3. Joan handed me a swab.

"For the port on the bag," she reminded me. I swabbed the spot where the vitamins would be injected into the bag. Then I inserted the syringe into the bottle of vitamins.

"Just push it about halfway down, and pull it back. See? You've got the vitamins in the syringe." Joan smiled, as I injected them into the bag. "You did it. Now add the other vial."

But this wasn't Jay I was injecting, I thought; it was just a bag. Anyway, he seemed to be dozing, for which I was grateful. Joan took the needles away from me. "These need to go straight into the sharps container." I didn't have a proper one, so I found an empty Tide detergent jug. She screwed the lid down tightly.

I attached the tubing to the bag, then into the pump, where I'd previously changed the batteries. It didn't end there. The tube had to be primed, the pump had to run a test on itself, buttons had to be pushed.

The PICC line had to be prepared. This was a thin tube that had been inserted into one of Jay's veins to carry the TPN. One of its ports needed to be flushed with the saline, and a blood thinner had to be injected.

Joan could see me struggling. "Remember to unclamp it.".

I bit my lower lip.

Jay opened his eyes. "You're doing fine," he murmured. I smiled at him gratefully. "Almost there." I took a breath. "I hope."

With the tubing attached at last, everything was ready. It had taken at least fifteen minutes. After a while, with practice, I managed to get it down to about seven. All the while, my spouse, not usually renowned for his patience, kept encouraging me.

The visiting nurses tended to come first thing in the morning, because we lived close to town, and they covered a wide geographic area, so some of their other patients were miles away. This meant that for the first seven days, I could ask them to watch me while I gained confidence in my abilities as the medical expert who could give Jay his nutrition every day.

After a week, the frequency of nursing visits was reduced, and I had to manage on my own. They told me that if I needed assistance, I could always call the VNA and they'd put me through to someone who could help.

Within days, though, Jay was getting frustrated with the fact that he felt tied to the pump for the whole twelve hours it took to get his daily nourishment. He was expecting a visit from two old friends.

"I can't let them see me like this," he said. "They'll think I'm sick, or something, chained to this damn tube."

I bit back a smile. Jay would not allow his friends to feel sorry for him.

"I wonder if you could have it at night?"

The nurse registered surprise when I asked her, but admitted there wasn't any medical reason why not. So, we changed the regimen, and Jay, who wasn't particularly restless when he slept, became accustomed to taking his tube into account overnight.

His two Yale classmates flew in from Texas and Florida, each hoping to boost the other's morale during what they knew would be their last chance to see Jay. They sat in the living room as I explained that he wouldn't be able to get out of bed to see them. I could see the shock on their faces. They'd only ever known him as the energetic man he used to be.

Yet as I closed the bedroom door, and left them to it, I heard laughter as they reminisced and teased each other. After forty minutes, sensing their friend was tiring, they said goodbye, Terry blowing his nose on a large handkerchief. Even Jack, normally in charge of his emotions, had tears in his eyes.

In mid-November, only ten days after he came out of Dartmouth, Jay was admitted to the local hospital with suspected pneumonia. When they let him out again it was with an oxygen supply. I was still at the hospital when it arrived, so Heather, who'd come to see him, stayed at the house and got the briefing on how to use it.

At first, Jay didn't want it, but the doctor told him it might be useful any time he wanted to concentrate, since it would provide an extra shot of oxygen to the brain. It would help him have enough breath for talking or moving around, too.

Fred took one look at the machine and decided it was disturbingly loud. He wheeled it into our closet and snaked the green hose out of the door, up the wall, across the door jamb, and into the bedroom. The closet and bedroom doors could be shut to make it completely silent for Jay.

❧ ❧ ❧

Jay had been fed intravenously for some weeks now, with me setting up the liquid food, adding the vitamins, connecting it all to a pump, and then to Jay. As I slept next to him, the shump, shump, shump of the pump provided a steady but sinister backdrop to my sleep.

He was taking in nutrition and calories intravenously,

but his appetite was still very poor. He would try to eat, but could manage only a quarter of a peanut butter sandwich, or a cup of beef broth. He wasn't drinking enough, but I figured he was getting plenty of liquid through the TPN, and at least he seemed to be gaining a pound or two. No one had been able to weigh him, of course, because he spent all his time in bed.

Jay was finally rescued from his nausea by Dr. Sanderson, head of palliative care and hospice at the VNA. She turned out to be a whiz at pharmaceuticals. When she first became his chief doctor, she'd wandered around to the passage where I kept the meds, with the schedule for administering them, neatly arranged in rows on top of chests of drawers. I had to give Jay pills eleven times a day, and was becoming increasingly stressed in case I made a mistake.

"Wow," she said. "I'm pretty sure he doesn't need all these."

She picked up the bottles one by one and scrutinized the labels. Every so often, murmuring something to herself, she put a container aside. I waited, wondering how he would manage without them.

"This heart medication." She held up a bottle. "It can cause nausea, you know. I'll check with his cardiologist to see if he can do without it."

"But... he has to have it or he'll..."

Dr. Sanderson looked at me. "At this point, I'd say Jay's comfort is the most important thing, wouldn't you?"

"Well, of course," I stammered. "But..."

"I won't cancel anything without checking with the cardiologist. But Jay's not exerting himself much now, so I don't think his heart is in danger of being over-stressed."

By the time she'd finished, she'd cut the number of medications almost in half.

"I'll give you a prescription for a different anti-nausea tablet I think will help. Maybe now *you* can get some sleep."

Days before Thanksgiving, Dr. Sanderson came to see Jay. She asked him about his appetite, and he told her what he was eating, exaggerating slightly to make it seem like he was managing to eat quite a bit.

"Today, I had banana and toast for breakfast, and yesterday I had a peanut butter and jelly sandwich for lunch and some pasta for dinner." He didn't mention how tiny the portions were. A couple of bites of banana, half a slice of toast, and a spoonful of pasta.

"That's great." Her voice was upbeat. "Sounds like you're doing better. So, the nausea's abated?"

"Kind of."

The doctor scrutinized him with a question in her eyes.

"I don't think the problem's nausea, precisely," I answered for him. I had some idea of what the issue was because we'd talked about it. But it wasn't something he'd want to admit to Dr. Sanderson. "I think it's more that Jay's *afraid* of getting nauseous. Sort of like with pain. The fear of it is worse than the thing itself. Same with the nausea."

"Is that right, Jay?"

He nodded.

"Well, give it a little more time. I think your confidence will come back."

As she was putting on her jacket in the hall, she turned to me.

"I'm worried about his appetite," she said. "As a rule, we only keep people on TPN for four weeks, and he's been on it for nearly five by now. Yet if he's not eating on his own, it's tricky."

I shivered. What would happen to Jay if he wasn't getting his nutrition?

She read my expression correctly.

"It's possible he's not hungry because he's absorbing his food intravenously," she murmured. "I'm going to reduce the TPN and see what happens."

My heart lurched. I didn't want to think about the

inevitable consequences if she did that and he still wouldn't or couldn't eat.

"Try not to worry." She gave my arm a gentle squeeze. But how could I not?

Chapter 22
Anticipatory Grief

One reason, perhaps the main reason, why I wouldn't give up on my relationship with Jay, was because I blamed myself for my father's death. I believed that if I'd been less naughty, tried harder, known more, he might not have died.

Since I never voiced this thought, no one disabused me of it, so I was an adult by the time I realized what the emotional impact of my mistaken belief was. Only then did I learn that most people who lose a parent when young tend to have depression as adults. Not only that, but the fear of being abandoned by someone you love can be life's chief motivating force for some people.

It was for me.

"Is Daddy going to die?" I remember asking my mother, after he'd spent months in bed, and several spells in the hospital.

"He'll be fine," she said, and because I wanted to believe her, I did.

That may have been the beginning of my ability to hold two conflicting ideas in my head simultaneously: he'll be okay, and—he will die. I was to use this skill every time I had to deal with the impending loss of someone I loved. I think it was F. Scott Fitzgerald who wrote that being able to hold two contradictory propositions concurrently was a sign of a first-rate intelligence. Maybe, but doing so produces incredible stress.

***

When my sister Susan died, ten years after Adam left home to live with his father, I had little time to grieve, because I was looking after her boys. So, I kept talking to my therapist, which helped pull me through.

Seven years after Susan's death, my oldest sister, Kay, developed late-stage ovarian cancer at the age of fifty-six. Once again, faced with the knowledge that this was sure to be terminal, I suspected the most helpful thing for Kay would be to keep encouraging her to hope. She lived much longer than anyone expected.

I never felt I was lying to her or to Susan when I told them things would work out the way they were supposed to. Perhaps I was deluding myself, too, but I don't think so. I just kept using that mantra and hoping for the best, even if the best might be a peaceful death.

Nine years later, my mother succumbed to a stroke followed by a heart attack when she was ninety-one. She'd done her level best to live as long as she was needed by the family. I expected sorrow to hit me hard, but I'd done everything I could for her, and we had no unfinished business between us.

Jay's illness was following much of the same trajectory as those of my father and sisters, and to get through, I would have to encourage him and myself to hope for the best even while expecting the worst. This time, it wasn't a case of visiting dying siblings or parents in another country; this meant facing the reality of the situation every single day.

❖ ❖ ❖

I thought Jay didn't realize how sick he was, but I could tell, from seeing the first scans, and after the first meeting with the oncologists, that nothing could save him. I would be abandoned once more. Although I behaved as if aware he would die when it came to practical things—checking that his will was up to date, talking to the doctors about what would happen—he and I rarely discussed death itself. We both acted as though there was always hope.

And yet, the certainty that Jay would leave me for good surfaced now and then in my tearful responses to relatively trivial events. When the hospital chaplain came to the house, she sat down near me and simply held my hand while I sobbed.

"I know I shouldn't be crying." I blew my nose on a tissue. "He's still here and I should be living in today."

"There's no should," said the chaplain. "It's called anticipatory grief, and you're absolutely allowed to have it."

I didn't want it. The only person who'd ever been able to console me, who'd always consoled me, was Jay, and I couldn't ask him to deal with my distress over his impending death. I'd have to grow up and cope with my sorrow without him.

Thirty years before, when we were separated for six months, Jay had kept a journal, almost a long letter to me, which I didn't read until recently. He'd had a kidney infection, and while feverish, had a dream.

"... *I dreamed about you last night, darling. It's sort of fuzzy, but it had to do with how calm you are in a crisis. I dreamed that you were sick, in the hospital, and I was caring for you. Your only concern was for me—that I shouldn't worry about you, that you would be fine....*"

Now the positions were reversed, and his concern was to support me in his sickness.

After he died, I found a note in Jay's now-shaky

handwriting, beginning, *"I've known for some four to five months that I'm going to die..."* Reading it, I realized he'd been determined to protect me while he was alive, and to make life as easy for me as it could be, in the circumstances. This only confirmed that he loved me and made me miss him more.

He hid the knowledge from me, and yet I wasn't deceived. I knew because he asked our lawyer to come over to make changes to his will, since it had been made some years ago, before we had grandchildren.

I knew because we slept together every night, and he would fall asleep holding my hand. I knew because he told me, so often, that he loved me and always would. I knew because he thanked me for all I was doing for him. I knew because he kept telling me I was the love of his life.

He went so far as to try and plan for my future. "If anything happens to me," Jay began. "I want you to get married again."

I raised my eyes from the book I was trying to read. We were sitting on our bed, and he was leaning back on the pillows while I sat at the foot, keeping him company. Since his diagnosis, I hadn't had many chances to relax.

The cancer attempting to take over his body had made Jay thinner and younger-looking again, and his handsome face now wore a solemn, even noble, expression.

Meeting his pale blue eyes, I laughed, hoping I would sound convincing. "You have to be kidding," I explained. "Men are such hard work!"

He may have looked hurt for a second, but I think he liked my answer. We'd always acknowledged that, while we weren't perfect, we were perfect for each other. Scrambling up the bed, I kissed him. "You're the love of my life, and that's that," I said. "Besides, you're going to be fine."

Neither of us believed he'd be fine, but this wasn't the time to talk about it. I rested my head against his bare chest, listening to the steady thump of his heart. Together we drank in the gorgeous vista before us. From behind the distant hills, the late afternoon sun was streaming across Lake Sunapee into our bedroom. It was going to be a beautiful sunset.

Chapter 23
Giving Thanks

Jay had his last infusion of TPN on the Tuesday of Thanksgiving week. He was relieved he wouldn't have to have it anymore, but he still wasn't hungry. I tried to make sure he drank some milkshakes made with full cream milk to add calories. He wasn't able to finish a whole one, so I would take them away with two-thirds of the shake still in the glass.

The family was arriving to spend the holiday with us. I wasn't looking forward to it because it would be another "last" for all of us. Amanda and Heather had told me they would take care of the cooking, and I was delighted to let them. Looking after their dad was a full-time job, and although I bought a turkey, roasting it seemed like an impossible task.

I knew I couldn't manage to have the whole family staying at the house. Even with plenty of rooms, the chaos of eight adults and six children would wear both of us out. So, I booked our daughters into a nearby ski lodge with an indoor pool, so their kids could work off some energy.

Understandably, Jay wanted to get out of bed to spend Thanksgiving with the rest of us. He shaved himself with his electric razor, and I helped him on with one of his favorite flannel shirts, a plaid in autumn colors, which seemed appropriate for this fall festival. I combed his hair. His face was still sunken, and his clothes were much too loose on him, but he was happy to be doing something "normal."

Fred, solidly muscular, strained to heave Jay into his wheelchair, and from there onto the sofa, where the slippery leather surface allowed Jay to slide around until he was comfortable, and put his feet up if he liked. Enticing smells of turkey and pumpkin pie hovered in the air, but I didn't feel hungry, knowing he didn't either.

The children laid the table and put out cranberry sauce and some rolls. The roasted bird was sitting out on the counter, ready to be carved by the most adept in the family, Barb, Amanda's wife.

"So, what have we got?" asked Jay. I wasn't sure what he meant. "Because I think I'll have some turkey, stuffing, cranberry sauce, gravy, and vegetables."

I didn't care if he was just saying it to be sociable.

"Whatever Lola wants," I said. "Lola gets," chimed in Fred, who'd heard me say it before.

"Just a tiny bit of everything," I told the girls, who were bustling around in great excitement, getting in each other's way as they all tried to prepare a plate for him. I found a lightweight tray and we arranged Thanksgiving dinner on a salad plate to look as appetizing as possible. All thoughts of sitting at the table were abandoned by the adults, who came to perch around Jay, their plates on their knees, as he slowly worked his way through the small, but complete, dinner.

I hid a smile when I noticed he'd left a roast parsnip on the side of the plate. He'd never liked parsnips. Cut off from me by a flock of excited adult children, Jay caught my eye and smiled. Even at death's door, I could see my Jay in his eyes and blew him a kiss.

Until that moment, I hadn't been sure he would live

until Christmas. Suddenly, everything had changed.

"I guess we'd better buy a Christmas tree tomorrow," I decided. "So this bunch," I waved an arm toward the grandchildren, "can decorate it."

Chapter 24
Christmas

On the day after Thanksgiving, I sent the men of the family out to find a Christmas tree. In the event that Jay's miraculous return to eating was a flash in the pan, I wanted to have at least a little Christmas immediately.

"It doesn't have to be superb. Pretty good will do fine. Just buy the best one you can see," I said, as Fred and Bertie left the house.

Some while later, letting a blast of icy air through the front door, they pulled a beautiful Norway spruce into the house.

Adam had put the tree stand in a corner from which he'd cleared the side tables and an armchair. Jay was sitting with his feet up on the red leather sofa, tucked in with a cozy fleece throw, and propped up by the pillow with a map of New Hampshire embroidered on it.

As the men adjusted and readjusted the tree to make sure it was straight, they'd check with him, looking for his approval. They knew that this Christmas, they had to get it right.

Someone had found the huge box of ornaments in a dark corner of the basement. Adam and Bertie hauled it up the stairs and into the living room, and I asked them to position it where Jay would be able to see it.

The grandchildren were hovering in the neighborhood of the tree and sofa, waiting impatiently to begin decorating. They'd never trimmed our outsize tree before, only the ones in their own, smaller, homes. The minute I lifted the bright green lid off the scarlet box, they crowded around it, craning their necks like baby birds and reaching in.

"Wait," I said. "I'm going to give each of you one bauble at a time to hang on the tree, or it won't be fair." A murmur of disappointment was quickly suppressed as I began to hand them out.

"We got this one in Leningrad in June, remember?" I looked at Jay. It felt like years ago.

"St. Petersburg," he corrected me.

"Here's the one from our first Christmas together," I handed a flying Plexiglas angel to Natalie. She headed over to the tree to hang it up.

"What's this one?" Ellie held up a blue ball with a painting on it.

"That's from the trip I took to Poland with Fred and Bertie for my mother's eightieth birthday."

The patriarch looked on, occasionally asking a child to bring an ornament over for him to inspect.

Near the tree, Heather was surreptitiously moving the baubles to higher branches or spacing them more evenly. Jay winked at her when he spotted her rearranging a sparkly *New Millennium 2000* silver ball, knowing this daughter liked things to be just so.

Outside, the lake was slowly disappearing from view as the sun set and the sky darkened. Bertie and Ned, Heather's husband, were stringing the fairy lights around and around the tree. Someone made hot chocolate for the grandchildren, to tide them over until dinner, and finally, with a last adjustment of the lights, nine-year-old Max was allowed to turn them on.

"What do you think?" asked Fred.

All heads turned toward Jay. He was gazing at the tree, the tiny lights twinkling in his eyes.

"You know," he said, poker-faced. "I think you might hang that one a touch higher up."

A moment's shocked silence ensued.

"Only kidding," he grinned. "It's perfect."

We breathed a collective sigh of relief, followed by a gust of laughter. It was so reassuring to be teased by Jay.

❖ ❖ ❖

He liked to celebrate the holiday with panache. Although we staggered visits from our daughters and their families between Christmas and New Year's Day, the general format was the same each year. To begin with, Jay insisted we provide at least four to five gifts per person. Having six children, two spouses, and six grandchildren, meant presents for fourteen people or up to seventy gifts.

Jay would buy some of them when we traveled, often purchasing six identical things, partly so he could bargain with the vendor, something he loved to do. I teased him that he'd been a market trader in a previous incarnation, as he began by offering 50 percent of the asking price.

While he pretended to walk away, I would make an apologetic face at the stallholder. In the end, both my husband and the shopkeeper looked delighted when the deal was closed. The former had his discount, the latter his sale. We had started our Christmas shopping.

This year, in Russia, he'd bought fur-lined leather gloves for the boys, placemats and napkins for the daughters, nesting matryoshka dolls for the grandchildren—including an unlikely Spiderman set for Max. That left a lot of things still to buy.

Thank God for online shopping. I had no hope of traveling to the mall in Concord, about forty minutes away, or even to Hanover, which took about half an hour. With someone to look after Jay for only three hours, I would barely have time to walk around the shops, never mind finding and buying gifts.

I did, in fact, try to shop one day, but the weather was so bad that only one lane of I-89 was open. I saw cars that had spun off the highway and into the wintry landscape of the center median.

Normally, I would have called the emergency services the minute I had a phone signal, because reception was sketchy in this part of the world. I could see flashing lights up ahead, which let me know the police and fire trucks had already been summoned. Someone's Christmas would be spoiled, I thought.

After an hour's driving, I'd only gone about two-thirds of the way, so I took an illegal U-turn through the median, tears of frustration stinging my eyes. My few hours of freedom had been wasted.

I scanned the Internet, looking for things that might please the family, and satisfy Jay, too. He needed to feel part of the gift-giving. I printed out pages of gift suggestions for his approval.

Delivery should be fast, and we had a whole box full of wrapping paper and shiny bows in the basement. I began to think I might conceivably be ready on time. But the packages didn't arrive. I'd get an email saying they'd been shipped, but they didn't show up. I checked at the post office on my daily run up to town, but only a handful of small parcels turned up there, and I was expecting many more.

I'd ordered comforting micro-fleece throws and pillows for our daughters, who all needed time to relax. The boys got tire grips to help them navigate the ice. Bertie, who liked to cook, had asked me, tentatively, for a KitchenAid mixer. Although he was only twenty-three, he took after his mother, Susan, in his enjoyment of cooking, and I was certain that if we gave him one, he'd use it.

"A mixer?" Jay's eyebrows were raised in surprise. "It doesn't seem like much of a present."

"Remember Bertie's chocolate-orange mousse?" I answered.

"Oh, that's right." He smiled. "Great idea, then."

And still, nothing arrived. Eventually, only days before Christmas, I tracked the packages online to find that they seemed to be close to us, yet they'd never quite made it. It was true the little road that led to our house was covered in snow, and some icy patches had formed there, but if the man who delivered Jay's medical supplies, the visiting nurses, and I were able to drive in and out, I was betting the UPS trucks could handle it.

I was wrong. Toward the end of one grayish afternoon, a delivery truck got stuck in our driveway. After several calls, I arranged with UPS that they'd phone from the main road, and I would head up in the pickup to retrieve the packages.

❋ ❋ ❋

Christmas passed in an exhausting blur. The children came up, and they took care of the housework and most of the cooking, but I still felt wiped out at the end of each day. As for Jay, he stayed cheerful throughout.

"You can fool some of the people all of the time." He smiled wearily.

But he wasn't fooling me.

Chapter 25
Money, Money, Money

Knowing very little about our finances, I felt I ought to get to grips with them sooner rather than later. As I began to understand the balance sheet, I realized now wasn't the time to try and sort everything out, so I decided on the priorities and did what I could.

Since Jay's bank account was in his name, not mine, I set up online banking to make life easier. I started by paying the bills electronically so I didn't have to sign checks.

Although we never discussed his death directly, he made sure I knew where to find the life insurance papers, which ensured I'd have enough to live on. I breathed more easily once I was certain I would have some income. It wouldn't be sufficient to maintain the kind of life we lived now, but I was happy with my small house and small car. There might even be enough to travel.

I caught myself and blushed, though no one was around to see me. How could I be thinking about life after Jay while he was still here?

* * *

Lake Sunapee Bank was a small local institution, where everyone knew Jay by name and looked forward to his regular visits. The first time I went in on my own, clutching a sheaf of checks to deposit, I handed them across the counter to one of the tellers, Shannon, together with a deposit slip.

"I'm sorry, but we can't accept this." Her expression was sincerely apologetic.

"Why?" I asked. "Have I filled out the form incorrectly?"

"No, it's just... you're not allowed to make deposits into Jay's account."

"That can't be right. I'm not trying to take money *out*— I want to pay some in. Why would it matter *who* did it?"

"I'm not sure, but those are the rules. I wish I could help."

My anxiety and frustration with my whole situation came bubbling up like hot lava. I was conscious that the bank personnel hadn't seen much of me over the years. I had my own account back in Fairfield, which had facilitated the transfer of money to Fred and Bertie when they were away at college, and I'd never changed it.

Now I was here in person, I had ID, and they knew who I was. I felt as though Shannon were adding a shovelful of hot coals to the volcano inside me. I didn't want to alienate the people I needed help from, so I didn't erupt with heat— I burst into tears.

"Oh, dear." Shannon's voice was full of concern. "Please don't..." She left her till and came around to my side of the counter. The only other customer stared as the teller led me over to the personal banking section and sat me down. She glanced around and found a box of tissues which she passed to me without a word. I grabbed a handful and wiped my eyes, but I couldn't stop crying. All the pent-up feelings of the last few weeks were pouring out of me.

"Let me see what I can do. You sit and take it easy for

a minute."

I sat, blinking my tears away and staring at the dust motes dancing in the shaft of sunlight streaming through the window. Outside, the roaring wind had blown the clouds out of the sky and was swirling brilliantly colored leaves into the air, giving a lively look to the deserted main street and the tiny local radio station across the road. I closed my eyes for a moment.

"OK." Shannon broke into my incoherent thoughts. "I've deposited the checks. But you're going to need your husband to add you to the signatories in order to carry out any more transactions."

I blew my nose and looked up at her. She dragged a chair over so she could look me in the eye.

"What does that involve?" I said.

"It's not difficult. He just has to come in and sign the forms, and you're good to go."

"You don't understand. He's in bed and I don't know when he'll be well enough to come in here." I felt tears welling up again. Jay was too sick to leave the house, a fact beginning to come home to me now.

"I'll be right back." Shannon disappeared into the manager's office. She re-emerged a few moments later. By now, I'd stopped crying.

"You'll need a power of attorney," she announced. "Michael Forrest can organize it for you."

I struggled to focus. Michael Forrest? This was the trouble with being in a small town. Everyone knew everyone else and assumed I did, too.

"The lawyer?" she prompted.

Of course. He'd drawn up our wills a long time ago.

"Jay's our favorite customer, you know," said Shannon. "We just love him."

I tried not to tear up again. "Me, too."

* * *

The bank staff continued to follow his progress and to help me whenever they could. They filled out the paying-in slips, helped me organize direct debits, handed me pieces of candy from the bowl on the counter, and generally treated me like a long-lost relative. And I counted on Jay's financial adviser, his accountant, and the lawyer to hold my hand.

Chapter 26
Late January

I sat looking at Jay sleeping in his hospital bed. A half-inch tube stuck out of the side of his chest, draining something resembling fruit punch from the area around his lung. We were several liters into it, and samples had been sent to the lab for testing. His breathing had improved somewhat, but I was aware that this fluid, ascites, signaled a major deterioration.

We'd come in the day before for a CT scan, scheduled because his breathing had been getting worse. They discovered his right lung had collapsed.

As the day wore on, Dr. Sanderson stopped by to visit. Jay was pleased to see her; she'd always give him straight answers.

"What are the options?" he asked as she parked herself on his bed. I hovered nearby, where I could read her expression as well as hear what she was saying.

"If we drain the liquid, the lung should re-inflate, and you ought to be fine."

He mustered a smile. "Let's do it."

"Once it's done, you'll feel a lot better." She put a hand over his and squeezed gently before getting up to leave. "I'll keep an eye on things," she told me. "Try not to worry."

There'd been talk of taking him to Dartmouth, but Jay didn't want to travel. He preferred to stay in New London, where they continued to remove the fluid. While he was dozing, I'd been watching the process for hours, waiting for the fruit punch to slow down and stop. I refused to think about sitting at Susan's side as this same dangerous liquid drained from her lungs only days before she died.

Every so often, a nurse would bustle in, check the patient's vital signs, write down the number of milliliters drained, and dash out again. Staff who knew Jay from previous visits—not only recently, but from old injuries like broken legs and elbows—kept popping in to find out how he was doing. A woman came in carrying a tray with a cup of tomato soup and a sandwich, which sat on the trolley next to the bed until she came to collect it again.

Outside, white flakes had begun to fall, swirling against the black night sky, the light from our window bouncing off the feathery crystals. I couldn't afford to stay too late. I'd been driving our scarlet pickup truck to and from the hospital. But digging it out of drifted snow wouldn't be any fun.

Sitting next to Jay, I felt useless. There wasn't anything I could do to make this go faster. I took the opportunity of texting the family, focusing on the fact that their dad would be coming home soon. Finally, Jay told me he was going to take a nap again, and asked me to go home. "I'll be okay," he assured me.

"I know you will." I amazed myself. How easily this lie came to my lips.

I left for home some minutes after seven, had some soup and a few Triscuits while watching part of an Agatha Christie movie on TV. I couldn't concentrate on Poirot and his clues, so I gave up and fell into bed by ten. I expected to feel lonely, lying there without my husband at my side, but I fell into a dreamless sleep and slept until nearly nine. I needed it.

By the time I reached the hospital the next morning, they were preparing to insert another drain because the lung had collapsed again.

The doctor on duty could tell I was beginning to feel the pressure. He walked me into the corridor so as not to disturb Jay, who was pretending to look at the newspapers I'd brought him.

"It's possible the fluid accumulated from congestive heart failure," he said, running a distracted hand through his hair.

"But?"

"But it's probably the cancer. If the lung keeps refilling, you have choices to make."

My mind went blank. I didn't want to make decisions. They weren't mine to make.

❈ ❈ ❈

January 28

A new doctor came into the room the next day.

"Well, it is cancer," he announced without preamble. He had evidently skipped the bedside manner class in his medical training. "The lab report shows malignant cells in the fluid. There's a small tumor on the pleura."

My mind flashed back to Susan. Small meant nothing, I knew. Small was still deadly.

I stood up from the chair I was in, beside Jay's bed, to hold his hand, the one with the IV in the back of it.

"They want you to go to Dartmouth," said the doctor.

I think he expected us to cave and say, "Okay." But we had questions that I was having trouble formulating.

"They can put chemotherapy drugs directly into the

pleural cavity," the doctor clarified. "But that has to be done at DHMC."

"How long would he have to stay there?" I asked.

"A day or two, I expect."

"And how much longer would it give me?" asked Jay, like a man with no time for obfuscation.

The silence seemed to go on and on. I don't remember the answer.

❋ ❋ ❋

Jay would trust only Dr. Sanderson to tell him the truth. We needed her to explain what she and the hospice team were able to do if he chose to go home without treatment.

She described what her team and the volunteers could do now Jay was officially on hospice. I focused on the news that we'd be getting a lot of extra care and help. They gave me a folder of information for carers. One item stood out. A bright-pink piece of paper, supposed to be prominently displayed, which announced, for the benefit of medical staff, DNR. Do not resuscitate.

I should have asked Jay what he wanted, but I already knew. Because I couldn't stand looking at it, I stuffed the thing into a drawer. Yet like Poe's *Tell-Tale Heart*, it haunted me.

"How long do I have?" he asked Dr. Sanderson.

She thought he had around three months, which took us to the end of May. It could be less, but he was stubborn; he might last longer.

A small glimmer of hope struggled to rise. He was still eating. This was good, of course, but there were drawbacks, too. I hadn't made a peanut butter and jelly sandwich until recently—I'm English. Or tapioca pudding. Meanwhile, my spouse only wanted food from his wartime childhood.

I knew how to cook Campbell's tomato soup. Meatloaf

I could do. Mashed potatoes, frozen peas, roast chicken, canned peaches with ice cream. And more ice cream.

I didn't eat much of this myself. I'm a vegetarian. Still, as I grabbed another sachet of almonds from the pantry, I was happy he was eating again.

The doctors were amazed, and I marveled at the resilience of this man.

The night before, they'd moved him to DHMC, and at the hospital, he'd had a toasted cheese, bacon, and tomato sandwich that I bought at the café, and he ate all of it except the crusts.

Now, in another waiting room at Dartmouth-Hitchcock, I was waiting for Jay to come out of surgery where they were inserting a PleurX catheter in his right side. This was a sort of tap, they explained, which could be opened twice a day to let out any fluid that might have accumulated. With it, he would be allowed home. I thanked heaven for the visiting nurses who would deal with this, but soon found that this job, too, would fall on me.

✳ ✳ ✳

Through all of this, the children and I kept in touch by phone, or more often, by text messages. To begin with, Jay would take phone calls from the children, but as his condition deteriorated, he'd ask me to say he was sleeping, because he was too exhausted to talk.

In general, it was easier to text everyone at the same time, rather than to speak to each individually. I'd learned this early on, when one would feel left out if I called another first. Also, phone calls often raised more questions than they answered, I found. Texts ensured they all had identical information, simultaneously.

I tried to maintain an upbeat tone, both in my texts and as I posted regular updates on a website designed for this purpose. This provided an efficient way to let people outside the family know what was going on.

While her dad was in and out of hospitals dealing with the lung issue, Heather texted to say she felt sorry I was going through this alone, but of course, I wasn't. I had Jay. Life would be so much harder after he went.

He was the only one who knew how to make me feel better. He'd always comforted me when people I loved died, but the times when I thought I'd never see him again were incredibly hard. I would survive, but it would be tough.

Jay's hospital stay lasted a week, after which he was delivered home by an ambulance that got stuck in our driveway. Fred helped dig it out, and the snow kept falling. We now had almost two feet piled up outside, which painted a delightful picture and was a royal pain.

Meg Williams, the chief nurse assigned to our hospice team, came over one day and drew me aside before she left.

"We're going to need a hospital bed," she told me. "This one is too low for the nurses. It gives them backache."

No. No. No. Absolutely not. He's not going to die on some plastic-covered mattress with railings on the side just because they think it's more convenient. I won't have it. After everything I've done to keep him in his own bedroom, with his own bed? And how can I sleep next to him if he's in a separate bed? No. No. And no.

I didn't say that out loud, of course. What came out was:

"Let me see if there's a way we can raise his bed. Give me a day or two."

I appealed to Fred, who came through again. Since Jay's half of the bed had four legs rather than being supported on the bed frame, Fred built two sturdy boxes. Each was wide enough for two legs to stand on, with a raised lip around the top edge to stop them from sliding. We moved Jay over to my side of the bed using the method I'd seen nurses and EMTs use—sliding the whole sheet over with the patient.

Fred managed somehow to lift the legs and push the boxes into place underneath them, making the bed almost a foot higher. I didn't care that my side was lower. I still fell asleep holding Jay's hand.

❧ ❧ ❧

With his lung re-inflated, he was able to breathe fairly well without any help from oxygen. I knew that wouldn't last. The terrible choices we might have to make: to treat it or not, and quality versus quantity of life, were staring us in the face now. We knew the time had come.

Jay and I talked about this, and he decided not to have any further treatment—not that there was much available. He preferred to stay at home and feel reasonably well and comfortable, so he could enjoy whatever time he had. His determination to keep on being himself remained undaunted.

This included watching the Super Bowl, before which he made a bet with Bertie on the outcome. I'm not sure Bertie knew what he was betting on, since he asked me afterward precisely what Jay meant. He wagered the New England Patriots would win by seven or more points. Jay's parting shot as Bertie left was: "Make sure it's a *crisp* five-dollar bill."

Shawn, his personal trainer, was one of the very few people Jay would allow to visit when he was sick. His spirits would rise as he sat in front of the fire in his usual chair, while Shawn derided the Giants or Yankees and Jay poured scorn on the Red Sox and Patriots.

When he came to call in January, I saw the shock in Shawn's eyes as he looked at Jay, now thinner than he'd ever been. Still, not by a single word did Shawn let slip that his buddy was anything but his old self.

Afterward, in the hall, he asked me about the prognosis. "I'm afraid it's not looking hopeful." What else could I say?

"I'll pray for him," said Shawn, a church-going man. "I wish I could do more."

"This visit has done him so much good." I meant it. "You helped him feel like a regular guy again—and all prayer is welcome."

Jay didn't believe in prayer, but knowing people were thinking about us and doing what they could, helped sustain us.

❅ ❅ ❅

"What *is* that?" asked Jay.

I followed the line of his gaze through the picture window and out to the late twilight of a February sky. I couldn't make out anything unusual. There stood the pines, by the shore, with ragged branches that always made me wonder how much longer they'd survive. Yet they struggled and straggled on, not ready to give up the ghost yet.

Behind them, the sky was a deep, rich blue, sapphire dark. I'd seen the sky and the pines before. What could Jay see that I couldn't? He was lying in bed, as he had been, most of the time, for the last few months. I tried to put myself in his place. Of course. His vantage point was different from mine as I stood next to him.

I moved closer to the window, reminding myself yet again that I simply must remove the splash of resin that had hurled itself against the pane and wouldn't let go. The crescent moon floated above me, stark white between the branches. To the right of it, the headlights of a plane were shining, almost the same color as the moon.

"Just a plane." I turned back to the bed.

"Are you sure?" said Jay. "It doesn't seem to be

moving."

I looked out again. He was right. It didn't appear to be going anywhere, but maybe it was traveling toward us, head-on, so to speak. In which case, surely it would either start looking larger, or would turn away.

It didn't change. The headlights, almost looking like one, shone steadily on in the same place.

"It can't be a star," I said doubtfully. "It's much too big, and in any case, it's sort of lumpy. Perhaps it's a satellite."

Jay closed his eyes.

"I'm going to find out," I murmured, almost to myself. I would have called our son Bertie, the astrophysicist, but was pretty sure he'd have no idea what it was. He knew how to get to Mars but was clueless about the names of the stars along the way.

I Googled 'extra bright star,' and waited for the results to appear on my phone. Apparently, I'd picked the right thing to look for, because 'extra bright star tonight' came right up. I read on. Jupiter, as it turned out, a planet, not a star, was visible now together with its satellite moons, in the northern American continent. So that's what it was! That's why one of the 'headlights' looked slightly larger than the other. The smaller one was a moon, caught forever in Jupiter's orbit.

Jupiter, king of the gods. The most important one. Perhaps the small moon orbiting around it was Juno, I thought, goddess of hearth and home.

"Darling." I turned to Jay. "It's your very own star—Jupiter."

Jay opened his eyes and looked at me, then back at the sky, as if to check that I wasn't making things up.

"Aren't we lucky?" He smiled. "If the sky had been cloudy, we would never have seen this."

I went over and kissed him. "Very lucky." I kissed him again.

❊ ❊ ❊

Some days later, Jay was looking out of the window at the frozen lake where ice fishermen were drilling holes in the ice before retreating into their huts to escape the wind.

"I wonder what people will say about me when I'm gone," he said, out of the blue.

I thought for a minute. "Would you really like to know?" I asked.

"Sure," he nodded. "It would be fun."

"Well," I replied, slowly, "I just happen to have..." Jay raised his head, startled.

"What?"

"Um, a draft of your obituary," I said in a rush. "Would you like to see it?"

He gave me a wry smile and nodded. I went over to the computer to print out a copy.

Simon, one of Jay's business colleagues and a close friend, had written to ask, a few months before, how he might help. Whenever possible, if people volunteered, I tried to find something for them to do. So, I'd asked Simon if, when the time came, he wouldn't mind letting the people in their business community know.

Simon was, or had been, head of more than one professional group, and his mailing list and press contacts were extensive. Within forty-eight hours, I'd received an email from him with an obituary attached for my review. It was only November, and I wasn't prepared for that, but I'd read it, made a couple of suggestions, and then filed it away. Now, Jay wanted to see it.

He read the contents in silence, a slight frown on his face, and then asked me to hand him a pen from the bedside table. I found one lying between the tissues and the glass of milk he hadn't finished, and handed it to him, holding my breath. Would he like the obituary, or would it throw him into a depression? He'd managed to stay relatively cheerful until now, but reading this might bring his situation home to him in a different way.

I walked across to the armchair, where a fresh pile of laundry waited to be folded. I could fold without looking at him, but I would hear any sign of distress. The silence was broken by an exclamation. I dropped the towel I was folding and spun around.

"What's the matter?" I hoped it was nothing egregious.

"Well, this is all wrong." Jay sounded offended. "He's got the universities in the wrong order. He'll have to put it right."

He seemed to be taking it quite well, all things considered.

"Overall, though?" I asked.

"Not bad." He turned to smile at me. I saw sadness in his eyes, but it was fleeting. "Just make sure Simon corrects this, that's all. I mean, when you've been to Yale *and* Cambridge *and* the University of Vienna, *and* served on the boards of several universities, you want the facts to be right." He gave me a wink.

"Yes, darling, you do." I took the pages from him and looked at the frail handwriting decorating the margins. "We'll get it right. Don't worry about that."

Jay closed his eyes. I was almost sure he was pretending to be asleep.

I had the bleak sense we were moving at a pace both glacial and alarmingly fast to the end of our story.

Chapter 27
My Valentine

We fell asleep holding hands every night. Which wasn't easy because our mattresses were never on the same level. Yet we were.

I'd kiss his head and face, not wanting to irritate him. He'd turn his head and suddenly, a smooch. A veritable movie kiss. Tongue. He looked smug. He'd caught me by surprise. There was touching, lots of it. He would lie in bed exhausted while I rubbed his feet, a slow smile spreading over his face as he basked for a while.

The thing was, nothing else could come between us now. No trips to plan, no household repairs to see to, no bills to pay. All that was for later.

We only had whatever time there was. I took care of him and he looked out for me. He would ask the nurses if I was doing okay because he didn't think I'd tell him if I needed a break.

He was mainly right. I did tell him I had to go out for a few hours now and then, but I was happy just being alone with him. Awake, asleep, we knew the other was there. I was in love with him again.

* * *

Jay was never particularly good at remembering anniversaries, birthdays, or other important dates. In the early years of our marriage, he'd often show up from work late on Valentine's Day, clutching a bunch of bedraggled roses. They'd likely cost him a fortune when he bought them at Grand Central Station on his way home.

I tried dropping hints, preparing candlelight dinners featuring a lot of chocolate, but none of it seemed to register. He would leave cards on my pillow in the morning, of course. They rarely focused on the romantic aspects of true love, more on the kinds of things Jay would like to do with and to me when he got home—which wasn't necessarily bad.

Some years later, a Godiva chocolate shop opened in Grand Central, and with a flourish, he would produce decorative boxes of superior chocolates from behind his back. I still have some of the boxes, where I keep small mementos. Some years, we might have dinner out, but I had to make the reservation, or we'd never snag a table.

So, on the whole, Valentine's Day was a bust. I became used to it and bought my husband the kind of cards I'd have liked him to send me. He sent cards to our daughters, and later to our grandchildren. I would receive naughty ones from him, and was glad Jay still wanted to send them. Still, I pined for the huge bouquet or the tasteful piece of jewelry which, if the TV commercials were to be believed, other people were getting every year.

Now that he was ill, we obviously wouldn't be going out for dinner on Valentine's Day, but knowing this would be our last, I wanted to make it special. At times like this, I felt the lack of entertainment in New Hampshire more keenly than usual. Perhaps that's why there are so many barbershop quartets in the Granite State.

Leafing through the weekly paper, I came across a black-and-white advertisement showing a picture of a rose and a Valentine's card: *Let us sing a love song to your sweetheart. Home or office. Card, chocolates, photo and a rose included. Please call...* and they gave a number in Hanover. I called, and a harassed-sounding woman answered.

"Yes?"

"Do I have the right number for the singing Valentines?"

"Just a second. Jim!" she shouted.

I heard a rustling in the background as Jim made his way to the phone. He sounded delighted to have a customer, and I wondered whether the group would be any good. This all seemed very amateurish.

I told him Jay was sick and asked if they would come to our house, explaining that access wasn't always easy if the weather turned bad again.

"No problem," he told me. "We're used to it. When would you like us to come?"

"Any time is all right, as long as I have some notice, so I can make sure my husband's awake."

"When we've got all the orders, I'll work out a schedule, but you're definitely in for Valentine's Day itself."

One other question occurred to me.

"What sort of songs do you sing?"

"Well, we harmonize, so we can do songs like 'Sweet Adeline,' 'Yes sir, that's my baby,' 'Don't sit under the apple tree...'"

"With anyone else but me, yes, I know," I interrupted. "I think I just want something romantic."

"Leave everything to me," said Jim. "We won't let you down."

Hanging up, I felt I'd done my best to provide Jay with a memorable Valentine's Day. Still, I wondered, what was he going to do for me? When I'd given him his newspapers and made sure he was comfortable, I addressed the issue head-on.

"Darling," I started. "What are you going to give me for Valentine's Day?"

My poor husband looked stricken. I didn't give him time to think about it.

"How would it be if I went and found something nice for you to give me—say, from Harrington's?" Harrington's was our closest jewelry store.

Jay beamed. "Great idea. How about something for your charm bracelet?"

"Mmm," I kept my voice noncommittal. You have to be kidding, I thought.

One of the aides organized by the visiting nurses was due to come the next day, and despite blustery weather and a threatening snowstorm, she arrived right after lunch. I wondered whether to go out, because I was expecting a call from Dr. Sanderson to tell me what, if anything, could be done about the fluid in Jay's lungs.

I decided to venture forth since my chances for getting out of the house were limited, and I set off for Newport in the pickup truck, feeling safer because of its size and four-wheel drive. As I reached the main road, the first snowflakes began to fall, and by the time I pulled up outside the jewelers, the snow was blowing across the street in ever-thicker clouds and swirls.

I clutched my coat around me and leaned into the wind. I could barely force the shop door open, it was blowing so hard, but I managed, and stood blinking flakes off my lashes. The store was in an old bank building, stolidly surveying Main Street ever since Newport had been a thriving industrial town. The inside was gloomy, but a warm gust of air blasted me from above as I entered.

A couple of saleswomen were chatting behind one of the glass counters, which housed a surprisingly meager collection of jewels. The women glanced over at me, concluded I wasn't a particularly likely prospect, and resumed their conversation. I headed over to the opposite counter, where the rings were displayed. I had some idea of what I wanted. Something pretty, but not flashy. Something to remind me of Jay every time I wore it. Something I could wear all the time without feeling overdressed.

I studied rings featuring various gems—aquamarines, a pink gemstone of some kind, one or two with emeralds, and some yellow topaz. Nothing spoke to me. A gray-haired woman glanced up from the counter where she was hunched over a display, rearranging the items inside.

"Can I help you, dear?" she asked.

"I'm looking for a ring, but I don't see anything I really like." I was beginning to feel discouraged. There wasn't another jewelry store for miles, and I didn't have much time before I had to get back to Jay.

"Let's see what we can find. I might have something that's not on display." She walked me back to the rings by the door, and began to bring out trays from below the counter.

Then I spotted it. A stone the color of Jay's eyes, with two tiny diamonds flanking it, set in a white-gold band.

"What type of stone is that?"

"It's a blue topaz," she answered. "Though really, these are much nicer, don't you think?" She pointed at an expensive sapphire set in yellow gold.

I tried that on—followed by the topaz. I held my hand up to the light. The ring fitted perfectly.

"I'll take this one," I decided, handing over Jay's credit card.

"Are you sure?"

I nodded.

"Well, it looks lovely on you. Good choice." She smiled and walked over to the cash register. As she prepared the bill, laboriously writing out a description of the ring, I asked her if she would gift wrap it.

"It's for my husband to give me on Valentine's Day."
She gave me a pitying look.

"He's too ill to buy it himself," I explained.

❋ ❋ ❋

The barbershop quartet did us proud. The singers, in various shapes and sizes, arrived a few minutes early looking impeccable in their black suits, white shirts, and scarlet bow ties. I asked them to wait in the hall while I got Jay into a shirt.

"What the hell do I need a shirt for?" he grumbled. "You know I'll only get too hot."

He wasn't going to dress without an excellent reason, so I had to tell him I'd arranged a singing Valentine. It had been many years since I'd organized anything of the kind, and that had been a singing French maid I booked for my starchy Polish cousin who'd been visiting us.

My husband had enjoyed it much more than Stefan, who blushed furiously and tried not to look at the ridiculously long legs encased in fishnet tights, as their owner cooed into his face. Apparently, Jay was remembering the same thing and perked up visibly as I helped him struggle into a soft plaid shirt. Knowing a photo would be involved, I was wearing the hot-pink cashmere sweater he'd given me, with the aid of Heather, for my birthday.

"Did you order me a stripper-gram?" he asked, hopefully.

"Not exactly."

At that moment, the four singers edged their way through the door, followed by Fred, and overheard this.

"We could strip, but I don't think you'd want us to," one of them chuckled.

I could see my husband agreed.

The lead singer was carrying a long-stemmed red rose, which he presented with a flourish. The tall tenor with the elegant white hair and glasses leaned over and placed a bag of chocolate truffles on the bed, and yet another handed Jay a card. They'd asked me what it should say, and all I'd been able to manage was "Love always, G."

"I'm going to conduct," offered my spouse, raising a hand in readiness. The barrel-chested bass stared at him over his hornrims and told him in his deep voice that he was free to do so, but for their part, they would be ignoring him. The four of them chuckled at this witticism.

Arranging themselves in a line in front of the window, they swung into "Heart of my heart" (the 1899 version) and sang "Let me call you sweetheart," as an encore. Totally sentimental, and entirely appropriate, I thought, as I tried unsuccessfully not to cry. Jay waved his hand in time to the music, anyway, while Fred captured the scene on video.

"Time for a photo," announced the youngest singer, pulling a small camera from his pocket. He turned to Fred.

"Why don't you take one? Then we can all be in it."

Fred obliged, and when he'd finished, I checked the picture to make sure it did us justice. The singer pulled a tiny printer from behind his back and, plugging it into the wall, proceeded to print a four-by-six-inch photo right on the spot. Looking at it now, I can see how desperately ill Jay was, but his beaming smile reassured me that this was one of the best Valentine's Days we'd ever had.

His cousins in Minneapolis, seeing that snapshot of us, sent a message to say: "You can tell people are best friends when they're having more fun than it makes sense for them to be having." And it was true. Not only around other people, but when we were alone, too.

❋ ❋ ❋

The last book Jay read was the latest Jack Reacher novel by Lee Child. The author had been interviewed on a podcast, and I was intrigued to discover that part of the plot was set in the area of London where I grew up.

I ordered a copy, and when Jay noticed me holding it, he tried to claim it.

"Not until I've read it," I said.

When I wasn't looking, he took to hiding the book under his pillow or beneath the newspapers that littered his bed. When I eventually prepared to sit down and read, I noticed it was missing and began to wonder where I'd left it. As I hunted around, checking my bedside table, the shelves nearby, and even under the bed, I found myself thinking out loud.

"I can't think where I put it. Must be in the living room. I guess this absent-mindedness is what they call chemo brain."

Normally, this afflicted the patients, but it seemed to be catching. I almost never read in the living room, preferring to sit in the cozy armchair in our bedroom, where I could keep an eye on Jay.

I expected him to make some sort of comment on this, but he didn't reply. I turned toward him and caught the twinkle in his eye.

"You sneak!" I said. "Hand it over."

"I've no idea what you're talking about," claimed my spouse, affecting an innocent expression. The innocence clinched it.

He held it out with a grin, and it became a game he played with me until I finished the book and let him have it. I'm not sure he ever got to the last page.

Chapter 28
Early March

I was waiting for Dr. Sanderson, who was supposed to be at the house by nine that morning. I hoped to see her before our old friend Tom Sargent came at ten. Jay's old Yale buddy had accompanied him on his second trip to Europe as a student in 1957. They'd remained friends ever since. Jay was barely seeing anyone, so I was glad he'd agreed to this visit.

Tom had flown in from California the night before. His wife, Helen, had died from a re-occurrence of breast cancer only a month ago, and now that Tom was free to travel, he wanted to make this visit a priority.

Michele, the home aide who came to give Jay a blanket bath three times a week, was washing his hair with a special foam that didn't need rinsing out. He loved having his hair washed. I don't think it was the clean hair so much as the head massage that he liked.

He'd lie back, eyes closed, while Michele leaned over him, sometimes singing as she worked. Her songs tended to be the ones she sang to her toddler children, but this patient didn't mind. Michele soon became his favorite caregiver. Her Canadian Indian blood, as she called it, gave her a striking appearance, with an olive complexion and black hair.

She always projected an air of confidence and chatted in a way that kept him engaged with the world. She'd served in the army, she knew the current football scores, and Jay would ask her about her children.

I could hear her now, singing "Zip-a-Dee-Doo-Dah" off-key in the bedroom. It's lucky he's a bit deaf, I thought. I'd made myself a cup of tea and was trying to relax as I sat looking out of the window at the garden.

The chickadees, away for the winter, were back, looking for seeds in the partly thawed wetlands. Plenty of snow still covered the ground, but the driveway tarmac was beginning to reappear from beneath it at the front of the house.

My husband would never see it, though. I dashed away a tear rolling down my cheek. The list of Jay's "lasts" was growing longer, and I doubted he would ever leave his bed now. I kept churning these thoughts around as my tea grew cold.

❊ ❊ ❊

The hospice service had given me a booklet about what signs to look for as a patient approached their last days, but I couldn't make any of the descriptions fit Jay's current condition. A week earlier, I'd asked the chief visiting nurse, Meg, what she thought. Every day now, I was obsessing over any sign that today might be Jay's last. I couldn't rid my mind of the thought.

"A couple of weeks ago, Dr. Sanderson told me she doesn't know why, but she's having trouble telling him he only has three to six weeks to live," Meg said.

I tried to do the calculations in my head. Meg had told us this a week ago, and had heard it from Dr. Sanderson two weeks before that, which meant three weeks had passed already.

"Can you give me any warning?" I had to know.

"I'll do my best," she said. "But everyone's different. And Jay is tough."

Although my brain couldn't take it in, my body was telling me I was scared. I felt simultaneously enervated and bone-weary. To calm myself down, I'd been eating sweet things, which wasn't helping.

After Michele left, I ran over the activities for the day. Dr. Sanderson should be here any minute. Tom was due at ten. Jay told me he wanted time to see his old friend on his own, and I'd warned Tom not to stay too long. I knew he'd understand.

Someone knocked at the door, and as I rose from my chair, Dr. Sanderson walked in. She took off her furry boots and left them next to the front door. I peeked into the bedroom and saw Jay had dozed off, something he often did after his bath. That gave me a few minutes to ask her what I needed to know.

"I'll be able to give you a better answer after I've visited with him," was all she would say.

When we woke him, he was drowsy and almost incoherent, like someone trying to talk through their sleep. I'd not seen him like this before, and gave Dr. Sanderson a look.

"I think some oxygen might help," she suggested.

I found the cannula that delivered the oxygen and fitted it around Jay's nose.

Dr. Sanderson sat down on the side of the bed and took his hand. He seemed to realize she was there, and began to come to. I hovered nearby as she took his vitals, checked his leg, and listened to his lungs.

"How'm I doing?" asked my husband.

The doctor paused before she answered. "I think you're holding steady. How's the nausea?"

"That's fine," I interrupted, before realizing Jay needed to answer the questions himself. "Sorry, darling." I shut up.

"Pain?" she went on.

"About a three." Three out of ten wasn't bad.

"Good. How about that cough?"

The cough was still an issue. I gave him an over-the-counter expectorant, but he never got rid of the phlegm that kept collecting in his throat.

Jay looked at Dr. Sanderson. "Now what?" he asked.

She understood what he was asking.

"It seems to me you're doing okay right now, but I need to ask you how you'd like me to handle things if you have another emergency." She paused. "For instance, if your lungs cause you problems again."

The silence conveyed its own message. I needed clarity.

"Are you asking if he wants to go to the hospital if that happens?"

She nodded.

"No hospital," said Jay. "I want to stay here."

The doctor stayed a while longer, chatting about anything other than cancer. She had the answer she'd come for. On her way out, I asked her what the prognosis was now. She told me that when she first came in, his condition made her think it was a matter of days, but having seen him, she thought he might have weeks. I should have asked her for something more precise because after she'd gone, I kept wondering what she meant.

Less than one month? Or less than two?

When Tom arrived, Jay wanted some time alone with his visitor, so he could ask about Helen's death. It hadn't occurred to me he needed this first-hand report until I heard their low voices through the baby monitor, which I'd bought to ensure I could hear Jay, no matter where I was in the house. I'd forgotten it was on. Now I could hear him asking whether Helen had been in pain. I turned the monitor off.

In spite of that, they had a wonderful time. I'd found the letters Jay had sent to his parents almost sixty years before, when he and Tom were traveling around Europe. I brought them in, and Tom read them aloud, commenting and laughing with his old friend as he went.

I spoke to Tom before he left. He told me he could no longer sleep in the room where Helen had died.

Chapter 29
Mid-March

It was almost ten in the morning and Jay was still asleep. I thought the pain meds were responsible for his lethargy and wondered whether I should try giving him a different medication, designed to counteract it. The hacking cough was still shaking his frame at regular intervals. No wonder he was so tired.

I was torn between wanting him to drink more milk, one of the few things he would still ingest, and the worry that it was making his exhausting cough worse. I'd found a new brand of milk containing thirteen grams of protein, instead of the usual eight, and Jay seemed to like it, so I gave him as many glasses a day as he could drink. If I switched him to any other liquid, he wouldn't get any nutrition at all.

He was doing his best to stay alive, I realized. He knew if he stopped eating, it wouldn't be long before his body gave up. So, he would ask for food. A tiny amount, but enough to prove he was trying. He still wanted a newspaper. He found the *New York Post*, mainly pictures, the easiest to look at.

His sister, Judy, came to visit him. They talked about old times in the hour or so she spent with him. I'd discovered a trove of letters his mother had kept, some dated from his time at a Massachusetts prep school. In one of them, which I pulled out from the folder where I'd stored it, he mentioned Judy, who'd come to see him at school with his parents so long ago.

I think my friends must be crazy, he wrote, *if they think my sister's a babe. I've known her for 13 years, and I can tell you, she has a face that could stop a truck!*

Judy, still a very good-looking blonde, laughed as she always did. She was stoic, but I saw tears gathering in her eyes. I left the two of them alone to talk, and went to the dining room. I was attempting an almost impossible jigsaw, a dark Vermeer painting, with far too many pieces for someone seeking only to distract herself. I didn't need any more challenges right now, but every visitor or nurse's aide contributed a piece or two to the puzzle, and the darn thing was almost complete.

When Amanda came up with Barb and Heather a few days before Jay died, I was still, rather half-heartedly, trying to finish it. We were practically done, but the last piece had disappeared somewhere, and we spent some time on our knees, looking under the dining room table, even under the rug, to no avail. While we were crouched under the table, inspecting the floor, Barb walked in from the bedroom, where she'd been talking to Jay. She stuck her head under the table to find Heather and Amanda.

"Your dad wants you," she said.

The girls looked at each other, sudden apprehension showing in their faces.

We scrambled to our feet, and the girls straightened their shoulders as we trooped into the bedroom. Jay was awake and alert, and he smiled at them as they stood at the foot of the bed, looking like children who'd been caught doing something naughty.

"Hi, Dad," Amanda began. "You wanted to see us?"

"Just wondering how the puzzle's coming along."

"The puzzle?" Heather's face wore an anxious expression.

"The jigsaw," Jay clarified. "I thought you were almost finished, so I was expecting you to come back and talk to me."

"Well." Amanda's tone conveyed something like a question. "We're almost done, but we seem to have lost a piece."

"Oh?"

I recognized the irrepressible laugh in their dad's eye. It took a second for the girls to register the expression on his face.

"Dad, you haven't..." Heather registered disbelief.

"How could you have?" Amanda's indignation may have been fake.

"What, you think I have that missing piece?" He tried, and failed, to look innocent and affronted. "I've been here the whole time."

Barb was trying to make herself invisible. I was reminded that this was a trick Jay had been playing on his daughters since they were small. He'd walk off with a bit of the puzzle, and as they were looking for the last piece, he'd stroll up to the table, and put it into place, claiming he was the one who'd finished it.

The sisters broke into smiles.

"Dad, you're incorrigible." Amanda looked delighted.

"That's right," added Heather. "Okay, let's have it." She held out a hand.

"Darn," said Jay. "You found me out."

He put a hand beneath his fluffy blanket, and moved it around, searching. A frown creased his forehead.

"Come on, Dad," and "You can't fool us," came the chorus from the girls.

"No, I mean it—it's disappeared."

I stepped forward to help him rummage through his rather disorganized bedding. As I lifted a corner of the blanket, Jay spotted the piece and waved it in the air.

"Okay, what's it worth?" he demanded, and exchanged it for a kiss from each of the girls.

"Why don't you go and finish the jigsaw while the going's good," I suggested, seeing his energy flagging. "Dad can have a nap before he thinks of something else to drive you nuts."

Muttering about the treacherous nature of Barb, who'd stolen the puzzle piece on Jay's behalf, they wandered out of the bedroom. I straightened the bedclothes, and gave him a kiss.

"I'll be here at the computer if you need anything," I murmured. Jay nodded as he closed his eyes.

❀ ❀ ❀

Outside, the spring thaw had finally started. As the ice melted, it sounded like slow raindrops dripping off the little tin roof that Jay had put up above the bedroom door so he could hear the rain. He loved the sound, but wasn't able to hear it now, since he hadn't worn his hearing aids for a while.

To amuse him, I hung up a birdfeeder, the old one shaped like a lighthouse, together with a wire cage containing some suet, but after almost a week, the chickadees still hadn't found it. A local bear though, waking early from its winter sleep, showed up a couple of days later and demolished it to get at the birdseed, much to our amazement.

Sitting on my side of the bed, I wondered whether to wake Jay or let him doze. I believed he knew he was failing and all I could do was tell him I loved him, hold his hand as we fell asleep, and kiss him once, and twice, and how many more times?

❖ ❖ ❖

The days passed, too slowly and too fast. Jay and I spent most of the time alone, and I think we both preferred it that way. He was cheerful and comfortable, and still had his sense of humor. When I was slow handing him something one morning, because I had my hands full, he expressed the hope that I wasn't shirking my duty. He was smiling, so I was almost sure he was joking.

But by mid-March, one of his lungs had collapsed again, and the other was beginning to fill with fluid, making his breathing more difficult.

One Friday, the doctor came to check on her patient and stayed two and a half hours. She laughed with him and they traded stories, but out in the hall, she gave me a hug.

"I'm afraid he won't be here when I get back," she said.

"When's that?" I wanted her to tell me she was going away for a month's vacation.

"Tuesday."

❖ ❖ ❖

Forty-eight hours later, I contacted the children. I was sure Jay had barely days left, now. He'd been sleeping all the time and eating virtually nothing. Almost as soon as they had assembled, he roused himself to tell me he would have dinner at the dining-room table, and, what's more, he wanted steak, Caesar salad, and garlic bread.

Our collective jaws dropped in surprise. I understood immediately that he wanted to be at the head of his family one last time. Knowing he was too weak to make it out of bed, I improvised.

"Have the boys bought the steak I wanted?" he asked, at about five o'clock.

"Of course," I lied.

I ran into the den, where the kids were sitting with the television playing on mute in the background.

"Dad really does want some steak," I insisted. "You'll have to go and get some. Right now." I saw their dumbfounded expressions change into ones of hope. "Take a credit card out of my handbag. Filet mignon." And I went straight back to Jay.

I persuaded him to stay put, and we all had dinner in the bedroom, forming a circle of chairs around the bed, plates on our knees. He ate some of the meat—a dolls' tea-party-size portion. And some Caesar salad. And a bite of my garlic bread so he wouldn't mind kissing me. The children chatted among themselves and teased each other. Bertie suddenly realized that he, the youngest at twenty-three, was more than a quarter-century younger than Amanda.

"I've just figured this out," he began. "You're old enough to be my..."

"Stop!" shot back Amanda. "Don't even think such a thing, never mind say it."

They all burst out laughing, and although Jay couldn't catch everything they were saying, his smile confirmed that he was happy because we were able to laugh for a while.

❀ ❀ ❀

So much for dying on cue. The next day, of course, he was exhausted, but he recovered somewhat during the week. Michele, the nurse's aide, asked if she could come every day, including Saturday and Sunday. When, one day, she started to sing again, I hit on the thought of finding a song that Jay would be familiar with on the Internet—I hoped it might help her to keep in tune.

I chose Richard Harris, singing "Camelot," a favorite of his. Michele didn't know the song, but as it played, I heard a thin but determined voice coming from the bed. "Camelot," sang Jay. "Camelot. La-la-la-la, dah-dee-dum-dah..."

Michele had developed a slight crush on him, as had so many of the people from the VNA. She told me later that she and the other carers and nurses asked to look after him because of the relationship he and I had. They took care of very few patients who, faced with such a dire situation, laughed as much as we did, who teased each other or were visibly affectionate. We had no choice, really. Dealing with a disease like this was hard enough with a sense of humor. It would have been impossible without one.

Chapter 30
End of March

All the children came up again the following Friday, and tiptoed in and out of the bedroom as Jay slept on and off during the day. I went upstairs for an afternoon nap while Amanda kept watch on her dad. I came downstairs at twilight to the smell of bacon and the rustling of a box of Cheerios.

"Dad's ordered breakfast." Amanda smiled.

"Fantastic," I said. "Just not too much, eh? He can always have seconds."

He ate it. I think he was determined to show us, and perhaps the children most of all, that he loved us and wanted to live.

The next day, I encouraged them to fix themselves some lunch while I kept Jay company. I sat on my side of the bed, one leg tucked under me, writing. I didn't want to forget anything about Jay and our time together. I was wearing more or less what I'd worn every day for months, a pair of jeans and a sweater, and a chain around my neck that I could hang my reading glasses on. I still swiped a dash of lipstick on my lips every day, because Jay would notice if I didn't.

Jay's left hand was resting on my knee. His eyes were closed, and he was breathing peacefully, his mouth open. His skin was pink and healthy—he looked as though he'd fallen asleep on the beach. A morphine pump, attached to his abdomen, was clicking every few minutes as it pushed through another regular dose.

The catheter that had been draining fluid from his right lung hadn't been used since the lung had collapsed again some time before. I thought it must be three weeks, but time had become something elastic—now stretching, now springing back to take me by surprise as I tried to work out how much time had passed.

Jay was literally death-defying. Ten days before, he'd been so ill that Dr. Sanderson didn't expect him to last the weekend. I thought about how the kids showed up, fearing a deathbed scene, and he rallied enough to ask if he could get dressed and have a steak dinner at the dining room table.

I had to move; my hip was beginning to ache. Jay slept on, with a sound like a regular snore. The noise was comforting, so long as I didn't stop to think about whether it was a snore or something more ominous.

His pain seemed worse in the early afternoon, so when Meg came, she upped Jay's morphine. We called her back at about four-thirty, and she began to increase the dose again. Jay's breathing had become ragged and his oxygen level was around sixty-nine—critically low. The children stood around the bed. I was completely focused on Jay. I expect they were too.

Abruptly, he tried to raise his head from the pillow. He was struggling to say something. I gripped his hand tighter, straining to catch his words.

"Okay—let's go. Let's go," he repeated several times, and fell back, his strength gone.

His breathing was still distressed, and I looked at Meg with a mute question. Then I heard him take a breath in. I stood, paralyzed, waiting for him to exhale.

I glanced over at Meg again, and after a minute, she said: "He's gone."

It was true. I could see the blood ebbing from his skin, turning his face to creamy marble, something I'd never seen before on Jay's always ruddy complexion.

From one moment to the next, the love of my life was gone.

Amanda told me later that his last look was at me.

I hope he saw the love in my eyes, and felt it flowing from my hand to his. I hope he knew I'd been with him until the end.

❀ ❀ ❀

There are those who want to hang on to any vestige of the one who's died. They take care of the body, sit with it, mourn beside it.

I'm not that person. I didn't want my last memory of Jay to be what remained of his faded physical presence. I turned away from the bed before the image could burn itself into my eyes. One of the children, maybe more, hugged me.

❀ ❀ ❀

Through the window, a beautiful silver sun was sliding down the sky, soon to be followed by a lovely crescent moon with Jupiter floating nearby. I imagined myself as the moon, and Jupiter as Jay, keeping an eye on me. I knew he wasn't actually hovering there, but he was, and always would be, an indelible part of me. We had told each other so often over the last seven months that we loved each other. I felt he'd given me enough love to last my lifetime.

I left the bedroom, and without any conscious thought, began to trudge up the stairs.

Chapter 31
Spring Gardening

Before Jay died, he told me he wanted his ashes scattered at
Sunset Shores, our home by the lake. I understood why he
wanted to stay here. It was his heaven, and he loved it.

❦ ❦ ❦

"You can collect the ashes, extra death certificates, and the
newspapers any time."

I recognized the sympathetic professional voice of Mrs.
Tibbet, the funeral director, when she called me about ten
days after Jay died. She was a calm, friendly middle-aged
woman with a scrubbed-clean face and hair that had never
seen a curl, who peered out at the world through thick
round spectacles.

I didn't want to collect any of it, of course. Not the
newspapers, not the death certificates, and definitely not the
ashes. I avoided driving by Johnson's funeral home for
several days after Mrs. Tibbet's call.

Eventually, New London being a small town, my
errands took me past Johnson's and I turned in, trying not
to think too much about what I was doing.

After signing the forms to say I'd received the ashes, Mrs. Tibbet produced a pile of newspapers and a huge American flag, folded into a triangle and zipped into a transparent plastic bag. Jay's stint in the National Guard, fifty years before, entitled him to this honor.

I wondered what to do with it. I knew, even as someone born in England, that the proper way to dispose of the Stars and Stripes was to burn it. So, how to do it? I was pretty sure the flag had to be unusable, and this one was new. Perhaps I might donate it to the local college Jay supported, and they'd fly it.

I studied the Stars and Stripes doubtfully as I began to unfold it. I hadn't realized it would be so enormous. Before I'd opened it fully, it occurred to me that this flag, and others like it, were made to be draped over a coffin. It was far too big to fly on any building in town.

I saved one copy of the *Intertown Record* and left the rest to give to the children on their next visit. The death certificates were neatly filed in the portable filing box that accompanied me everywhere these days.

But the flag? I propped it up on the mantelpiece where it peeked out from behind the Chinese clay horse.

* * *

In early April, at the party we were having for Jay ten days after his death, I stared out at the view. Different every day, it was still wonderful, even with the couple of feet of snow that covered the whole terrace, including the two chaise longues and the dining set.

As the last guests were leaving, Dr. Sanderson asked about burial plans.

"He wanted to be scattered here," I told her.

Her warm gray eyes expressed concern. "I don't think I heard that," she said. "If I had, I'd have to tell you it's illegal."

My shoulders relaxed a little. I didn't want to scatter the ashes. Visions of them blowing back in my face with a sudden gust of wind, all too likely by the lake, had been haunting me. Which left me with the question of what to do with them.

I had to do something memorable for the children without frightening the grandchildren. It had to be what Jay wanted and something I wouldn't ever regret.

I worried at the problem for weeks, while the ashes sat, in the plastic bag with a zip-tie, inside a tasteful forest-green cardboard box with Jay's name and an identifying number on it. This, in turn, was housed in a non-biodegradable matching tote, with the words: *Johnson's Funeral Services, family-owned and operated for 100 years,* printed on it.

I wondered if it paid to advertise, as I stashed it on a shelf in the closet, behind my husband's tuxedo—all that remained of the racks of clothes he'd amassed over the years. I'd given everything else away within days of his death, some even before. If I hadn't, they might have become a permanent fixture I wouldn't be able to deal with.

Back in Connecticut, I talked over the problem of the ashes with my friend Katherine, whose spiritual outlook on life had been sorely tested once on being given a brass heart containing some ashes as an unconventional souvenir of a dead friend.

She told me about her unsuccessful attempt to get rid of the heart by throwing it into a tidal river where, to her dismay, it reappeared the following day. We sat by the same river and roared with laughter, wiping tears from our eyes. As she dropped me off at my house in Fairfield, I grabbed her arm.

"I've got it," I told her. "There's this cushion and I could put them inside..." I babbled on.

Katherine gently removed my hand from her arm and patted it. I realized I wasn't being quite clear.

"You'll be fine," was all she said.

Once in the house, I rushed upstairs to the bedroom. On the bed sat the cushion, covered with coffee-colored burlap and about the size of a large envelope, with the word "nest" embroidered on it in periwinkle-blue thread. The back was tied with a blue bow. I untied it and took out the smaller pillow inside. It was filled with feathers, which I disposed of in the trash compactor.

When I reached New Hampshire the next day, all the family were gathered. An almost palpable tension pervaded the air—even the children were playing quietly instead of making their usual racket. Helenka would have to leave the next morning at seven to be back in Connecticut for a dance recital. Fred was out being a best man at a friend's wedding. It was clear not everyone would be able to be present when we buried the ashes.

I bought some helium-filled latex balloons and some small cards. I gave one to each person and asked them to write a note to Jay on it. The children, seated around the dining table, concentrated on using their best handwriting as they wrote. The adults perched around the room, and when all the cards were ready, we tied them to the strings of the balloons.

Keeping them in a bunch, we wandered down the garden path, past Jay's little beach, and out to the end of the dock. Once there, I let the children hang onto them, and at a signal, they let the bunch go. I prayed the environmental consequences wouldn't be too dire.

We watched them rise into the sunset sky, across Jay's beloved lake, beyond the lighthouse, and on toward the mountain, until our eyes could no longer see the tiny speck. After Susan died, I'd devised this way of honoring the people I'd lost when I needed some ritual that might comfort Freddie and Bertie. And me.

❧ ❧ ❧

The next morning dawned sunny and serene. It was time to deal with the ashes. I realized they shouldn't be buried in the plastic bag because it would take a century to bio-degrade. So, I carried the pillow and ashes into the bathroom, offering up a silent apology to Jay, in case I spilled some. With this potential disaster in mind, my fingers trembled slightly as I tried to cut the zip-tie. My nail scissors weren't strong enough, so I found some office scissors in Jay's desk drawer, which seemed appropriate, somehow.

I made myself look at the ashes. Thank God there weren't any chunks of bone among them. I'd dreaded coming across a vertebra or two but, of course, that wouldn't make sense. Though the horrifying thought that a dog might dig up one of the bones froze my marrow. I forced myself not to think about what happened to the bigger bones. Surely if they'd been included, even ground up, there'd be more ashes than this.

No matter. I decided the cotton inner bag might be feather-proof, but probably not ash-proof, so I searched around for something else that would be bio-degradable. Of course. A brown Kraft envelop would be perfect, and I found a new one on Jay's desk. He was making quite a contribution to this.

I tipped the ashes carefully into the envelope, managing not to spill any. Then back to the desk for Scotch tape and the stapler. This package simply must not come adrift. I'd left some feathers in the cushion and now they came in handy. I filled in any spaces between the envelope and the lining with enough down to give the cushion a comfortable look. Just to be on the safe side, I stapled the inner bag too and eased the whole thing into the cover. Perfect.

The men in the family, meanwhile, had been busy digging a hole outside. I went out to check on them and stifled a smile as I took in the solemn masculine scene before me. They were measuring depth and width and working out what to do with the earth they'd dug out. Problem-solving, in fact. The best way for the men in my life to deal with grief.

Amanda and Heather, with grandchildren milling around them, were in the kitchen.

"Can I put in a chess piece?" asked Max, ten.

"Great suggestion," I said.

"I could add a backgammon piece." Amanda's question was almost tentative. This was a game she'd been winning and losing with her father since she was small.

"Sure."

She went off to find the set that was already missing a piece.

Heather had another idea. "How about Sudoku?"

Oh, dear. I'd given away all the books of Sudoku puzzles. Jay never bothered with them, preferring the daily challenge of those in the newspaper. *The Boston Globe*, much too liberal for him ever to read, was lying on the dining room table.

"Cut it out of the paper," I suggested.

Barb had brought back a coffee cup from Jake's. I thought about how Jay would go there every day for his favorite hazelnut version.

"Why hazelnut?" I'd asked him years ago.

"I don't like the taste of coffee," he explained. I smiled as I remembered.

Adam came in from the garden, trailing mud over the kitchen floor. "What about a golf tee?"

"With his clubs," I said, my mind on something I wanted to add, too.

I found an ornate silver goblet, one of a pair we'd been given as a wedding present by our best man, and walked down to the beach. I filled it with some of the sand Jay had used to build the tiny beach a couple of years before, and planned to sprinkle it beneath the tree we were going to plant.

We were as ready as we'd ever be. "All right. Let's begin."

I waited for them all to gather outside before I carried the cushion, the ashes nested within, out into the sunlight.

They arranged the totems along the low retaining wall and then stood around the hole. Abutting it was the young tree that Jay had asked for, in lieu of a memorial stone. It was a prairie-fire crabapple, and I felt planting a fruit tree right here was appropriate.

We were burying Jay in the plot of earth that had been his vegetable garden. He would continue to provide.

Epilogue

Only after Jay died did I give any real thought to how the love we'd lost had come back to life. All I clung to, as the months went by, was the certainty that I loved him again, not just in the "best friend" way I did as I contemplated divorce, but in ways that brought back memories of the time we first fell in love, forty years before.

Back then, I lived with a mixture of hope, anxiety, longing, joy, and the need to touch him. Those feelings echoed during his illness.

Like all those newly in love, I thought about him constantly. When he wasn't with me, I speculated as to where he might be, what he was doing. Over the years, I'd stopped thinking that way, and began to wonder where *I* was, what *I* was planning, what *my* life consisted of.

Yet during his last few months, he became my constant preoccupation again. Every thought, action, and conversation I had was about Jay. I did try to look after myself, too, but only to stay well for his sake. I don't regret any of it; it's just how it was.

I remembered the sudden elation when, years ago, we reunited after an absence. I might not have seen him for some weeks, and experienced a combination of relief and delight, as I saw him walking toward me along the concourse at Heathrow Airport. Those feelings mirrored the emotions I felt now, when I tiptoed into his bedroom several times a day and found him awake, cheerful, and pleased to be with me too.

One day, I'd perched on the side of his bed, trying to ignore the medical paraphernalia surrounding us, and reminded him of our first tryst, and that extra stolen day. He held my hand, his thumb stroking my knuckles, as his eyes searched my face and he smiled.

"We've had so many great days since then," he said.

I nodded, not trusting myself to speak. I think we were both wishing we might steal a few more.

The physical longing at the beginning resulted from an unquenchable need to be with him, to make sure he was still there. I yearned to lean against him, circle him with my arms and hold him to me. I had to hear his heart beating in his chest. I needed him to want me the way I wanted him. I'd wake up before he did and sit, watching him sleep, sure life offered nothing better than it did at that moment.

When he was sick, I needed to hear the regular thump of his heart for a completely different reason. Sometimes, sleeping soundly because the painkillers had done their job, he looked almost too serene. At those moments, I would sit, staring at his chest, waiting for it to rise and fall again, to reassure myself that he was still breathing. At times, the wait seemed interminable, and in the silence, I held my breath too.

The intimacy, which had dwindled over the years, became more important than ever. True, this wasn't the passionate euphoria of the first days of our romance, but the urgency to feel his skin next to mine was rekindled. Sometimes all we could do was hold hands as we fell asleep.

At other times, Jay would open his arms and I'd rest my head on his chest, always alert to any possible discomfort he might be feeling. With so many pieces of medical equipment connected to him, the thought of accidentally dislodging something was agonizing. I kissed him more than I had in the last two years combined. I had to, while I was still able. The inevitability of time passing weighed heavy.

The ups and downs of our London love affair were repeated now. Each time Jay appeared to improve, I'd come alive too. When he was in pain, though, or when I sensed things weren't going well, I had to fight my anger with the way life was going to separate us one last, irrevocable, time.

I wondered what had happened to Jay's anger, which seemed to have fallen away. Maybe it had been fueled by the drinking? Surely, now he was ill, he had every reason to "rage against the dying of the light," but if so, he overcame the urge. Perhaps, like me, he felt that time was short and best not wasted on negative thoughts.

The loss of control, too, reminded me of the early days. I understood then, as I did later, that I could do nothing to keep him with me. I was all too aware that no unexpected move to America, no trip to Hong Kong, no lunch in Chicago, would enable me to see him, ever again.

❖ ❖ ❖

In London, after we first met, we'd gone to see a theatrical revue called *Cole*. It was based on the life of Cole Porter, like Jay, a Yale graduate, so I thought he'd enjoy the performance. I knew many of the songs by heart, and one, in particular, always came to mind whenever we parted. *Every Time We Say Goodbye* talks about lovers who keep separating, which causes the world to change from a major to a minor key, with a corresponding change in the music. I'd always felt it expressed how I felt about our separations perfectly.

One evening, when I walked in to check on him, Jay lay dozing, lit only by the soft light of the bedside lamp. We were alone since Heather was sitting at the dining table distracting herself, as I sometimes did, with a jigsaw.

As I sat on the bed and took his hand, I gazed at his face, reduced by cancer to its essence. That song came unbidden to mind, and I sang it to him. He didn't stir, but his eyelids fluttered as if he might have heard.

I'd forgotten the baby monitor was switched on. When I walked out into the light of the living room, Heather had tears in her eyes.

Nothing altered the heart-stopping dread that crushed my chest at the thought of our final parting. All I could do was leave the room and howl in private.

❀ ❀ ❀

The only person that ever managed to comfort me when someone I loved died, was Jay. Now I would have to face his death, my greatest loss, without him to lean on.

I sat in my favorite reading chair, re-reading some of the letters he'd sent me decades before, and wondering whether doing so was only making me feel worse. And then I came across this, written a year or two before we married.

"I've had to share myself with other people in this life, but the next world is completely yours. Do you believe in an afterlife? I may have asked you that before, I've forgotten. I do, because I believe in the infinity of man's/woman's spirit… Does this make any sense? No matter, I believe that our love is infinite. You have always been a part of me."

I stared out of the window at the garden and felt peace course through me, knowing Jay would always be a part of me, too.

Acknowledgments

Many people have gone into the making of this book. I want to thank particularly the members of my critique group, who read patiently as I went through several drafts of the book. Liz Morten and the late E. Katherine Kerr helped me keep writing when my emotions got the better of me. Peggy Knickerbocker, Lori Stewart, C. Lee Mackenzie, and the rest of my critique group helped me get the book done.

Liz – you were there for me before and after the writing—I couldn't have done it without you. My dear friends, Margaret Rumford and Debra B, held my hand throughout.

My editors, Kim Caldwell Steffen in the US, and Doug Watts of JBWB in the UK, helped shape the words to make sure they could be understood on both sides of the Atlantic. Any mistakes in the book are my fault, not theirs.

Carol Dannhauser, my first writing teacher, author, editor, and friend, gave me helpful suggestions for improving the book. And WFWA writing friends Michele Montgomery and Priya Gill, offered me great feedback too. And my thanks go to Kiana Stockwell, my tireless intern, who helped me get the word out and reminded me when I needed to get things done.

I so appreciate the unswerving support of friends who believed in me and the book—who thought I had a story worth telling—and kept asking me when they could read it.

They know who they are. They're the reason I finally had to send it out to publishers. And I'm grateful for the members of my writers' groups, the *Writers' Rendezvous* and the *WritersMic*, and the *Monday Morning Write-in*, who celebrated every forward step along the way and commiserated with every step back.

Thank you to the midwives at Atmosphere Press who helped bring this work into the world. In particular, my editor Colleen Alles championed the book from day one.

Above all, I want to thank my readers, without whom a book is not a book.

Author's Note

Thank you so much for taking the time to read *Love's Journey Home*. If you enjoyed it, I'd be so pleased if you would leave me a short review on Goodreads or Amazon, or anywhere online. Reviews help other people find new books to read. And if you and your book club would like to read *Love's Journey Home*, I'd be delighted to join you to answer questions—in person, or on Zoom.

I'd love to stay in touch. You can reach me through my website www.gabicoatsworth.com or follow me on Facebook, Twitter, Instagram, and Goodreads. If you'd like to read more of my fiction and nonfiction, you can do so here. And if you want to find out when my novel is coming out, sign up for my email list to get updates and bonus stories.

Readers' Guide

1. What surprised you most about the book as you were reading it?

2. Do you believe in love at first sight?

3. Gabi and Jay met in the 1970s. Do you think the social changes of the time contributed to their instant attraction?

4. What effect do you think the frequent separations had on Gabi and Jay's romance? Does absence make the heart grow fonder?

5. Letters formed a huge part of the way Jay and Gabi really got to know each other though they were thousands of miles apart. Have you ever written a love letter? Do you have any love letters, either of your own or of an older generation? Do you wish you had?

6. Gabi left England in 1979, expecting to be away for six months. Would you like to do something similar?

7. How do you think the losses in Gabi's life affected her emotional journey?

8. What could she have done differently to improve the marriage? What would you have done?

9. Many people have experienced cancer and or alcoholism in their life, either directly or via people they know. If you have, how did that affect your reaction to the book?

10. Do you believe that this book has a happy ending after all, or is it tragic?

11. What about this book has stayed with you?

About Atmosphere Press

Atmosphere Press is an independent, full-service publisher for excellent books in all genres and for all audiences. Learn more about what we do at atmospherepress.com.

We encourage you to check out some of Atmosphere's latest releases, which are available at Amazon.com and via order from your local bookstore:

Sit-Ins, Drive-Ins, and Uncle Sam, by Bill Slawter

Black Water and Tulips, by Sara Mansfield Taber

Flawed Houses of Four Seasons, by James Morris

Words For New Weddings, by David Glusker and Thom
    Blackstone

*It's Really All about Collaboration and Creativity! A Textbook
    and Self-Study Guide for the Instrumental Music Ensemble
    Conductor*, by John F. Colson

A Life of Obstructions, by Rob Penfield

My Northeast Passage—Hope, Hassles and Danes, by Frances
    Terry Fischer

Love and Aspberger's: Jim and Mary's Excellent Adventure, by
    Mary A. Johnson, Ph.D.

Down, Looking Up, by Connie Rubsamen

About the Author

photo credit: Amy Dolego-Winton Studios

Award-winning writer Gabi Coatsworth was born in Britain and work brought her and her two children to America. Love was why she stayed, and that love, with its many detours, became the inspiration for *Love's Journey Home*. She lives in Connecticut in a cottage that's American on the outside, and English inside. If she's not reading, writing, or traveling, she'll be in her flower garden, wondering whether to weed, and holding a cup of her preferred beverage, strong English tea. The rest of the time she's working on her next novel.

9 781639 881505